MULTIPLY MINISTRIES

THE MUSTARD SEED TRIBE

LARRY WALKEMEYER

FreeMo
JOURNALS

In response to many requests for small group and Sunday school materials, Light and Life Publishing is pleased to present the FreeMo Journals. These books have been ideally prepared for any leader to facilitate discipleship in a small group setting, or for individual Christians to employ as a resource for their daily devotions.

The FreeMo Journals cover a wide variety of topics, but have been framed around the Free Methodist Church's Nine Strategies for whole church growth.

- Rev. Jay Cordova, Publisher, Free Methodist Church - USA

If you would like to purchase more issues of the FreeMo Journals please go to: www.freemethodistbooks.com

FreeMo

JOURNALS

MULTIPLY MINISTRY

THE MUSTARD SEED TRIBE

TABLE OF CONTENTS

INTRODUCTION

God looked at the big new world and the size of his human creation and commanded them to "fill the earth and subdue it" (Genesis 1:28). A tall order for a small couple. Thankfully, God in the phrase before, gave them the power and tactic. It was simple but potent - "Be fruitful and multiply". Multiplication was God's original game plan for expanding his kingdom.

Many years later, Jesus arrived and reemphasized this strategy of expansion. When he did, he bent down and picked up a seed that was only 1/64 of an inch wide, held it up, and said, "The kingdom of heaven is like a mustard seed, which a man took and planted in his field. Though it is the smallest of all seeds, yet when it grows, it is the largest of garden plants and becomes a tree, so that the birds come and perch in its branches." (Matthew 13:31-32)

Jesus was introducing his disciples to the multiplicative, viral nature of the gospel of the kingdom. It was as small, but as prolific, as the wild mustard plant which adorned the hills of Israel with its yellow flowers. Something miniscule could have a profound impact and become a gift to others far beyond its own seeming limitations.

Mustard plants are one of the most remarkable plants in God's garden. As a spice, mustard is only surpassed in importance by salt and pepper. It is one of the hardiest and most generative herbs. In the Southern California desert the Sahara Mustard plant has gone from obscure to prolific in just 15 years, causing desert dwellers to form groups in an attempt to halt its viral spread.

As followers of Jesus we are often tempted to look in the mirror at our own limited dimensions and envision the future based on the reflection we see. What can I do? How much can my ministry accomplish? How can our little church have an impact? How can we leave a significant legacy?

Answer? Multiply. One phrase God has been using to overhaul my thinking is this: "Mini is mighty if multiplied." I pastor a small church that has grown to 1000 in attendance. We have planted 19 churches nationally and catalyzed dozens of churches internationally, but I had missed my induction into what I will call "The Mustard Seed Tribe". I had majored in addition and not in multiplication. Our church had done good ministry but missed the best one.

Since I am a pastor, nearly all of my illustrations will be about the work of pastoring a large church. Forgive me for this. I realize most of you are not pastors, but it's my hope that you'll be able to learn from my stories and apply the same strategies and principles to your own life regardless of your context.

This book issues a call to embrace the place God has reserved for you in the Mustard Seed Tribe. This Tribe consists of passionate disciples of Jesus who believe multiplication of ministry is the means to significant kingdom impact. Mustard Seed disciples and leaders are those who have an understanding of the power of multiplication and have dedicated their lives and ministries to its deployment.

In the pages that follow I will introduce you to 13 important beliefs of the Mustard Seed Tribe.

CHAPTER ONE: SEED

WE BELIEVE JESUS IS
THE TRUE SEED OF
MULTIPLICATION.

GALATIANS 3:16 – "The promises were spoken to Abraham and to his seed. Scripture does not say 'and to seeds,' meaning many people, but 'and to your seed,' meaning one person, who is Christ."

My friend, Ralph, was a typical follower of Jesus during the Jesus People movement of the late 1960's. In 1971 God spoke to him in the middle of a crowded restaurant and directed him to Hermosa Beach to start a church. At the first meeting it was Ralph, his wife, Ruby, Carl their six-month old son and 9 other people. Ralph didn't know much about what to do, so he just preached Jesus. Jesus as Savior. Jesus as King. Jesus as Healer. Ralph discipled people around that same theme of Jesus. The church, named Hope Chapel, began to grow. It was an uncomplicated format with a strong emphasis on...you guessed it...Jesus.

Ralph began to sense a call to start other churches with this same focus - Keep it simple. Keep it about Jesus. Keep it about people. **KEEP IT ABOUT JESUS CHANGING PEOPLE'S LIVES.** They had started 29 churches when the Lord spoke to Ralph again. This time it was a call to leave his now mega-church and go start a new church. Ralph once more obeyed the voice of Jesus and went off to plant the seed of Jesus on the island of Oahu. Today Hope Chapel Kaneohe Bay is a thriving church that has planted many Jesus-exalting churches. But Ralph is no longer pastoring there because at age 67, in 2013, the Lord called him to plant Hope Chapel - Honolulu.

While I was at dinner with Ralph last month, he admitted, "When someone told me over 1000 churches had been birthed as a result of that first church in Hermosa Beach, I woke up in the middle of the night and thought, 'What if that's not true but I've been telling it to audiences?'" Consequently, a study was done to account for all the churches which trace their spiritual lineage to that first Hope Chapel. The result **WAS OVER 2300 CHURCHES ARE IN THE LINEAGE OF THAT FIRST HOPE CHAPEL CHURCH.**

Ralph Moore is now 70 and not stopping his emphasis on two things – Jesus and multiplication. Ralph would tell you, "The secret sauce is not a great strategy but a great Savior".

CONSIDER THIS: DO STORIES LIKE RALPH'S INSPIRE YOU OR DISCOURAGE YOU?

JESUS.

HE IS THE ONE WE WANT TO SEE MULTIPLIED

THE MUSTARD SEED WAS THE SMALLEST SEED KNOWN TO THE JEWISH GARDENERS OF JESUS' DAY. It was a common seed, unremarkable in every way, except perhaps for its diminutive size. It was a seed with multiple uses. Soaked in wine, the seed would release its spicy flavor which was craved by the Israelite palate. The crushed seeds were used as a source of oil for the lamps which illuminated the Jewish homes. Almost all parts of the mustard plant were (and are) edible.

Since before Christ, **THE MUSTARD PLANT HAS BEEN USED FOR HEALING PURPOSES.** It was first mentioned as a curative in the Greek's Hippocratic writings. In the form of mustard paste, it was used for general muscular relief and to help relieve toothaches. It also became known to stimulate appetite and digestion, help clear sinuses, and increase blood circulation.

When Jesus spoke of the kingdom of God being like a mustard seed (Mark 4:30, 31) he may have had himself in mind, the king of this kingdom. He may have been remembering the words of the prophet Isaiah in Isaiah 53:2,3 "...He had no beauty or majesty to attract us to him, nothing in his appearance that we should desire him... and we held him in low esteem."

JESUS WAS THE UNDERVALUED SEED who would grow up like a young plant, propagate, multiply then fill the earth with his offspring.

The Mustard Seed Tribe has a singular focus on the true seed – **JESUS. HE IS THE ONE WE WANT TO SEE MULTIPLIED.** If we are making a disciple, we want to see Jesus, not ourselves, replicated in our disciple. If we are leading a small group our first priority is not getting the vibe just right, it is seeing Jesus exalted. If we are running a ministry – whether youth or outreach or homeless or justice– we are seeking to see Jesus manifested. If we are planting churches, it not our brand, our band, our preacher or our label we are promoting. It is a profound encounter with Jesus. This is the only seed that we can trust to multiply.

It is this under-emphasis on the true seed which often leads to the dismal harvest we see in the ministry of Christians and churches. **WE PLANT A SEED OTHER THAN THE REAL JESUS, THEN PRAY FOR IT TO GROW AND WONDER WHY IT DOESN'T.** As Paul writes in Galatians 3:16 "... Scripture does not say 'and to seeds,' meaning many people, but 'and to your seed,' meaning one person, who is Christ."

CONSIDER THIS: WHAT ARE THE DISTRACTIONS WHICH DILUTE YOUR FOCUS ON JESUS? SOME MAY BE GOOD THINGS.

The apostle John won't allow us to miss the power of this one true seed – Jesus says, "I am the bread of life" (John 6:35); "I am the light of the world" (John 8:12, 9:5); "I am the door" (John 10:9); "I am the good shepherd" (John 10:11); "I am the resurrection and the life" (John 11:25); "I am the way, the truth, and the life" (John 14:6); "I am the true vine" (John 15:1). **JESUS IS WHERE THE LIFE IS.**

Jesus was speaking of the cross but also giving us a spiritual principle to minister by when he declared, "And I, when I am lifted up [the Greek here can also mean "exalted"] from the earth, will draw all people to myself" (John 12:32). **THERE IS A "DRAWING", AN ATTRACTION THAT HAPPENS WHEN PEOPLE EXALT JESUS** and not themselves, their ministries, or their churches.

I am reminded of the young boy in the church Christmas play who had one line to deliver, but when it was his time to shine, he forgot his one line. Thankfully, his mother was in the front row and began to whisper the line to him - "I am the light of the world," she hinted. The boy didn't quite hear her and softly murmured back, "What, mom?" A little louder, his mother replied, "I am the light of the world." With that, the boy straightened up and in a booming voice declared, "My mom is the light of the world!"

There is one true light and our message must not be forgotten, twisted, or diluted. The one seed we want multiplied is Jesus.

CONSIDER THIS: WHAT DO YOU SEE IN THE CHURCH THAT THREATENS THE PRIORITY UPON JESUS?

With that in view, we can look at two other ways Jesus uses the term "seed."

The first is found in the parable Jesus tells about the four types of soil we will encounter in our process of evangelism and disciple-making (Matthew 13:3-9, 18-23). In 13:19 Jesus says the seed is the "message of the kingdom." In 13:20 the seed is "the word." These are synonymous in the parable and identify the same thing

Jesus taught in John 8:32 "You shall know the truth and the truth shall set you free." Jesus identifies himself as "the truth" in John 14:6.

The "message of the kingdom," "the word," and "the truth" are each ultimately pointing back to the true seed - Jesus. **THE BIBLE, ALONE, DOESN'T SAVE US.** The Bible presents to us Jesus, the one who saves us. If we do not major on Jesus when preaching the Word, we miss the truth. We fail to pass on the seed. Too many Christians want to use their Bible to prove something to you instead of to introduce someone to you.

Jesus' second use of "seed" is found in the next parable he tells in Matthew 13:24-30. It is the story of the sower who plants good seed, but then an enemy sneaks in at night and plants weed seed. The servants are ready to pull up all the weeds but the master says, "No, wait until harvest because then it will be evident which is which." In the explanation of the parable Jesus makes this statement – "The field is the world, and the good seed stands for the people of the kingdom. The weeds are the people of the evil one." (Matthew 13:38)

Kingdom people are identified as "good seed." **THE TRUTH IS YOU ARE EITHER SEEDS OR WEEDS!** But we must be clear about WHY we are seed. It is not because of the life intrinsic in ourselves. It is rather due to our ability to carry the true seed. We become "people of the kingdom" only when the king moves into the castle of our lives. Multiplication DNA is not resident in our talents, gifts, intellect, strength, skills or sparkling personalities. It is only present in the true seed.

CONSIDER THIS: HOW AWARE ARE YOU THAT YOU ARE CARRYING THE SEED OF THE KINGDOM IN YOUR LIFE?

This is the apostle Paul's passionate plea in Colossians 1:27-28: "To them God has chosen to make known among the Gentiles the glorious riches of this mystery, which is Christ in you, the hope of glory. He is the one we proclaim…"

The mystery of the gospel is that **CHRIST, THE TRUE SEED, CAN LIVE IN AND THROUGH US.** It is this seed we proclaim and share with the world. This is the seed which will multiply.

As my friend Ralph Moore wrote recently in his blog: "Sick Christians chase fads. Healthy Christians stick to God's formulas and get on with life. They truly 'find themselves' as they imitate Christ."[1]

---

1   Ralph Moore. http://www.ralphmoorehawaii.com/ (accessed June 7, 2016).

THE FORMULA FOR MULTIPLICATION IS NOT THE NEXT CHURCH CONFERENCE, the newest model or the ensuing book. It is people who "find themselves" as they imitate Christ and who then overflow with his contagious reality.

My wife, Deb, is one of my heroes and a Mustard Seed Tribe kind of women. She carries King Jesus around with her wherever she goes. She's not a street corner preacher who nails people to the proverbial wall with a turn or burn message. She's just natural with people but always looking for a chance to plant the seed of Jesus.

Eight years ago, my wife and I started renting a 103-year-old house in Long Beach from a nearly retired university Art professor. It's a spacious old place in need of some repairs, but that fact is offset by a gorgeous view of the Pacific. God miraculously opened the door for us to rent it as we were ninth in the waiting line to rent it at its below-market price. As we moved in we inquired of the Lord, "What is your mission for us in this place?"

We didn't have to look far. Our landlord, Tracy, lives above the garage behind the house. Tracy can literally look down from her porch into our kitchen and tell you whether I'm having oatmeal or bacon for breakfast.

Now, that reality could be quite negative, except that Tracy has become our friend and even an extended member of our family. Tracy has been a "spiritual" person but her understanding of Jesus was underdeveloped. Deb wasted no time in "planting the seed" of Jesus into Tracy's life. Through numerous acts of kindness and conversations the trust level began to build. Then Deb hosted a women's group focusing on Jesus. She chose a book study on "Surprised by Hope" by N.T. Wright. Tracy came and began to encounter the true seed.

CONSIDER THIS: WHO IS YOUR TRACY, THE PERSON OR PEOPLE YOU HAVE ACCESS TO SHARE THE SEED WITH AND HAVE IT MULTIPLY?

Gradually Tracy began coming to our church. Next she began helping with our Community Center Theater program for under-resourced children putting her set design skills to good use. Her friendship circle in the church continued to grow.

A few months ago Deb and I were in the baptismal water as Tracy publically professed her lifetime commitment to Jesus as her personal Lord and Savior. Tracy still has questions, but one fact she is certain of – she's met Jesus and her life changed. The seed of Jesus has sprouted and is producing new fruit in her life.

Three weeks ago our small groups pastor told Deb, "Did you know Tracy wants to go through our small group training? She wants to share Jesus with others like herself." Deb's spiritual lineage is multiplying.

THE SEED IS JESUS.

QUESTIONS TO CONSIDER:

1. Do stories like Ralph's inspire you or discourage you?

2. What are the distractions which dilute your focus on Jesus? Some may be good things.

3. What do you see in the church that threatens the priority upon Jesus?

4. How aware are you that you are carrying the seed of the kingdom in your life?

5. Who is your Tracy, the person or people you have access to share the seed with and have it multiply?

CHAPTER TWO: VIRAL

Tab. III.

WE BELIEVE IN MULTIPLICATION MORE THAN ADDITION.

MATTHEW 13:8 "Still other seed fell on good soil, where it produced a crop- -a hundred, sixty or thirty times what was sown."

KINGDOM MATH MAJORS IN MULTIPLICATION, NOT ADDITION. Sadly, few followers of Christ understand the difference between the two.

One simple metaphor for distinguishing the two is this: Addition happens when you have children. Multiplication occurs when grandchildren are born. You can't have grandchildren unless you first have children. But having children doesn't guarantee grandchildren.

My wife Deb's dad came from a family of 18 children. 70 years later their reunions are huge. Five generations are there, eating fried chicken together. But Deb's dad only had two girls. Deb and I only had one biological child, her sister had none. Our daughter is married but with no children. Our Harshman family gatherings are tiny. Now that Deb's father has passed away there are two generations with seven people there. **IF NO MORE CHILDREN ARE BORN, OUR FAMILY REUNIONS WILL SOON CONSIST OF SOME PHOTOS IN A SCRAPBOOK, LIKE MORE AND MORE CHURCHES I KNOW.**

Addition is vital. Addition is introducing someone to the life-changing reality of Jesus as their Savior and Lord. It is planting this seed of Jesus into the heart of an individual ready and willing to believe. **THIS SEED PRODUCES NEW LIFE**, a young plant, that never existed previously. This is glorious addition, but not yet multiplication.

CONSIDER THIS: HAVE YOU EVER THOUGHT DEEPLY ABOUT THE DIFFERENCE BETWEEN ADDITION AND MULTIPLICATION?

In Matthew 13:22-23 Jesus contrasts two different kinds of plants – "The seed falling among the thorns refers to someone who hears the word, but the worries of this life and the deceitfulness of wealth choke the word, making it unfruitful." The seed added a new plant to the garden but it never matured to multiplication.

Matthew 13:23 describes the second kind of plant – "But the seed falling on good soil refers to someone who hears the word and understands it. This is the one who produces a crop, yielding a hundred, sixty or thirty times what was sown."

The phrase "times what was sown" underlines the dynamic difference between the two plants. **THE SECOND PLANT MULTIPLIES ITSELF BY PRODUCING SEED,** which causes it to yield up to 100 times itself.

The Mustard Seed Tribe includes disciples passionate about "times-ing" themselves, about not just adding to the kingdom but adding something that multiplies. This tribe of believers understands the viral nature of the kingdom and wants to see it unleashed in their slice of the world.

THE MUSTARD PLANT IS NOTORIOUS FOR BEING A VIRAL PLANT. "Viral" in this context means a plant that spreads rapidly and widely via a multiplication of itself. Depending on the variety of mustard plant, one plant can produce up to 6,000 seeds, though 600 is more typical. These seeds are dispersed by diverse means. If these seeds find good soil they reproduce a new plant that in turn produces thousands of seeds.

In Southern California one invasive form of mustard, the Sahara Mustard, has proven how viral mustard can be. In 1998 one acre of Sahara Mustard was located in the Mojave Desert portion of the California desert. Just eight years later, through the power of multiplication, the plant had spread to approximately 32,000 acres.[2]

If you were going to make a one-minute movie and try to get 10 million people to watch it, you probably wouldn't film two brothers interacting as the younger brother bites his older brother's finger. Yet, over 840 million people have viewed "Charlie Bit My Finger" on YouTube. Why? It went viral.

"Viral" in this context means the video was so engaging it leveraged people's online and offline social connections to spread rapidly and widely. There wasn't a ten-million-dollar ad campaign on TV to drive viewers to the movie (an addition model). It was a no-cost social recommendation in which one person told a friend who showed it to a different friend who shared with another friend (a multiplication model).

One of my friends who is a global expert on the church recently told me he believes that church growth as a primary goal has been a key limiting factor to the spread of the church in western countries. Please understand, he is an advocate for church growth; he cheers for mega-churches. What he has recognized, however, is that **WHEN A CHURCH MAJORS IN GATHERING BIGGER AND BIGGER GROUPS OF PEOPLE INSTEAD OF PRIORITIZING SENDING SMALL GROUPS OF BELIEVERS TO START NEW WORKS, THEN THE OVERALL GROWTH OF THE CHURCH IS HINDERED.**

2   Craig Dremann, *Desert Exotic Invasive Mustards in the USA.* http://www. ecoseeds.com/mustards.html (accessed June 8, 2016).

CONSIDER THIS: HAVE YOU EVER HELPED ADD SOMEONE TO THE KINGDOM?

David Garrison has written on the subject of global viral movements. He has researched these Church Planting Movements around the world and has developed a description: A Church Planting Movement is a rapid, exponential multiplication of churches within a given people group or population segment. He has seen this happening around the world. [3]

Ed Stetzer and Warren Bird, however, pointed out in 2012 – "Based on lots of research--ours and others--we've found that of the 34 Western, industrialized democracies in the world, there is no Church Planting Movement among majority peoples in any of them."[4]

OUR ADDITION IDEA OF CHURCH-THE BIGGER, THE BETTER-HAS DISTRACTED US FROM GOD'S MULTIPLICATION IDEA FOR THE CHURCH-THE MORE, THE BETTER. We must add to the church, but we must ensure that addition is not an end game but seeks to serve the greater purpose of multiplication. The church cannot go viral without such an emphasis.

CONSIDER THIS: HAS A PERSON YOU DISCIPLED HELPED SOMEONE ELSE INTO THE KINGDOM?

With that in view, we can look at two other ways Jesus uses the term "seed."

The first is found in the parable Jesus tells about the four types of soil we will encounter in our process of evangelism and disciple-making (Matthew 13:3-9, 18-23). In 13:19 Jesus says the seed is the "message of the kingdom." In 13:20 the seed is "the word." These are synonymous in the parable and identify the same thing Jesus taught in John 8:32 "You shall know the truth and the truth shall set you free." Jesus identifies himself as "the truth" in John 14:6.

The "message of the kingdom," "the word," and "the truth" are each ultimately pointing back to the true seed - Jesus. **THE BIBLE, ALONE, DOESN'T SAVE US.** The Bible

---

3   Ed Stetzer, *"Viral Churches: Thinking about Church Multiplication Movements in the West, Part 1 of 8,"* Christianity Today, February 14, 2012, http://www.christianitytoday.com/edstetzer/2012/february/viral-churches-thinking-about-church-multiplication.html (accessed June 8, 2016).
4   Ibid.

THE BIBLE, ALONE, DOESN'T SAVE US

presents to us Jesus, the one who saves us. If we do not major on Jesus when preaching the Word, we miss the truth. We fail to pass on the seed. Too many Christians want to use their Bible to prove something to you instead of to introduce someone to you.

At our church, Light & Life Christian Fellowship – Long Beach, in 1999 we reached a proverbial fork in the road between addition and multiplication. My wife Deb and I came to Long Beach in in 1991. I had just read the most popular book on church growth. It emphasized that if you wanted to attract "customers" you needed an abundance of convenient parking. When I stood in our parking lot and counted a total of 39 parking spots, I said, "Thanks a lot, God! **HOW CAN WE HOPE TO GROW WITH THIS KIND OF CUSTOMER PARKING?"**

Nevertheless, we grew rapidly, even winning an award for being the fastest growing church in our denomination one year. At 700 people we knew we had to make a decision regarding our strategy for the future. The question was whether we would relocate into larger facilities and add more to our existing church or would we remain in our current facility and seek to send people out the door to start a new church.

As we prayed, God gave us a vision from Ezekiel 47 of the river flowing out of the temple bringing life to wherever it flowed. To this point we had been a "lake" church, where the priority was on people flowing in and staying in. Our goal had been to gather more people around one pastor in one place to grow our one church bigger. We felt God calling us to become a "river" church, where people would flow in but we would then help many of them flow back out to start new ministries and churches elsewhere.

We chose multiplication. We opened the gates to the dam we had built and have watched as leaders, ministries and groups of people began to flow out to the world around us. The result has been far beyond anything we could have accomplished through addition. Last Easter, over 6,000 people were in churches started by Light & Life and our 39 parking spaces.

As Robert Schuller famously said, "You can count the seeds in an apple but only God can count the number of apples in a seed." Addition is counting the seeds in your apple. Multiplication is planting the seeds in your apple. **YOU DON'T GET TREES BY GATHERING THE SEEDS INTO A LARGER AND LARGER PILE.** You must release your seeds and plant them.

1,048,576 disciples. This number startles me, then convicts me, then convinces me to major in multiplication. I have had this kind of math explained to me many times with various analogies attached to it. Yet, recently, I have become deeply gripped by this number and the concept behind it. Let me explain.

1,048,576 IS A VIRAL KIND OF NUMBER AND CAN EITHER STRIKE US AS VERY SOVEREIGN OR QUITE RANDOM OR RESERVED FOR THE ELITE. It can feel sovereign, like something God elects to do by his own volition on rare occasions. Conversely, it can seem random, like an unusual combination of factors coincidently coming together to create an extraordinary result. Or, it might feel elite, like you must have the gifting, intellect and anointing of the apostle Paul to consider such a significant number. Yet, this number is not reflective of any of these explanations.

Unlike the viral videos on YouTube, **THE VIRAL EXPANSION OF THE CHURCH USUALLY HAS SOME YEARS OF SMALL, FAITHFUL DISCIPLE-MAKING BEHIND IT.** The wildfire sweeping through China, India, and parts of Africa was at one time a few disciples "rubbing sticks together" as they learned the multiplicative principles and power of disciple-making; learning that "mini is mighty if it multiplies."

1,048,576 is an attainable number in 20 years of disciple-making. Most readers, including myself, are apt to cynically dismiss such a number. But what if we ask the question, **"HOW MANY OF YOU BELIEVE YOU COULD FIND ONE PERSON WHO WANTED TO BE DISCIPLED AND DISCIPLE THAT PERSON FOR A YEAR?"** How impossible does that seem? Perhaps you haven't done it yet, but do you believe you could do it?" Most of you reading this would answer, "I think I could do that. One a year doesn't seem too far-fetched. Definitely possible."

CONSIDER THIS: WERE YOU TRAINED TO MULTIPLY YOURSELF?

Now, if you could do it for one year, could you do it with another person the next year? You should be able to reply, "Probably. Yes, I think I could". Now, would you believe me if I told you, "Just do that; **JUST ONE DISCIPLE A YEAR FOR 20 YEARS IN A ROW AND YOU HAVE THE POTENTIAL OF MAKING 1,048,576 DISCIPLES** over the next 20 years. Or you might do the same thing and only make 20 disciples." Wait, what!?

There's a big difference between over a million and only 20. Why the discrepancy? The gap is **THE DIFFERENCE BETWEEN ADDITION AND MULTIPLICATION.**

If you disciple a different person each year for 20 years you will have trained 20 disciples. This is great work, better work than most American Christians ever accomplish. But is that the goal? Or is the goal to reach as many as possible for the kingdom?

IF, HOWEVER, YOU TRAIN YOUR DISCIPLE TO MAKE ANOTHER DISCIPLE AND YOU SEND THEM OUT THE NEXT YEAR TO DO WITH ONE OTHER PERSON WHAT YOU HAVE DONE WITH THEM; THEN AT THE END OF YEAR TWO THERE WILL FOUR TOTAL DISCIPLES – yourself and three others. If all four of you now embrace this disciple-making, multiplication DNA and determine to take just one person to disciple them in this brand of disciple-making; then by the end of year three there will be 8 of you. Repeat this for year 4 and there will be 16 of you. Doing it again in year 5 will result in 32 disciples.

32 disciples after five years is not bad, but it's not earth shattering and certainly is a long way from 1,048,576. But just keep doing what you're doing. Year 6 will see 64 disciples. Year 7 shows 128 disciple-making disciples. Now you are to the number that was in the upper room at Pentecost.

Keep doing it and **BY THE END OF YEAR 20, THROUGH THE POWER OF MULTIPLICATION, THERE WILL BE 1,048,576 DISCIPLES.** This is amazing. Go ahead, check my math. That is viral growth. This is mustard seed living.

If I asked you, "Can you make a million disciples in your lifetime?" You would say, "I wish, but no way!" But if I asked you, "Can you make 20 disciples who believe in and practice disciple-making?" You would reply, "With God's help, I think I can!"

Now I see a few—okay, several—of you rolling your eyes at the naiveté of my calculations. I feel your doubt. I have the same question you do: "If it's doable, why hasn't it been done?" I heard similar multiplication formulas as I was going into ministry. Forty years later, I've not really seen it, and I know people have been trying.

The truth is **DISCIPLES ARE REAL PEOPLE WHO HAVE SETBACKS, WHO LOSE THE VISION, WHO GET DEFEATED BY THE DEVIL, WHO BREAK THE CHAIN.** Also the fact is, we fail to do a thorough job of training and instilling this multiplication DNA into the generations we equip. It's a slow, faithful process that seems insignificant (mustard seed size), so we are easily distracted to what seems more exciting, visible, bigger.

While 1,048,576 would be super and is theoretically and theologically possible, it's not the goal; the power of multiplication is! If we only actually hit 10,000 in our spiritual "downline" instead of a million plus, I guarantee **WE WILL ENTER HEAVEN REJOICING AT HOW GREATLY GOD HAS USED US.**

CONSIDER THIS: DO YOU BELIEVE DISCIPLES, MINISTRIES AND CHURCHES CAN ACTUALLY MULTIPLY? HAVE YOU EVER SEEN IT HAPPEN?

Addition is great; multiplication is greater. Viral is the greatest.

QUESTIONS TO CONSIDER:

1. Have you ever thought deeply about the difference between addition and multiplication?

2. Have you ever helped add someone to the kingdom?

3. Has a person you discipled helped someone else into the kingdom?

4. Were you trained to multiply yourself?

5. Do you believe disciples, ministries and churches can actually multiply? Have you ever seen it happen?

CHAPTER THREE: FAITH

Tab X.

WE BELIEVE GOD IS ABLE TO DO MUCH WITH LITTLE.

MATTHEW 17:20 "He replied, 'Because you have so little faith. Truly I tell you, if you have faith as small as a mustard seed, you can say to this mountain, 'Move from here to there,' and it will move. Nothing will be impossible for you.'"

Mustard Seed faith moves mountains.

Tre was a close friend of mine in college. Her smile was legendary on campus. It lit up her gorgeous face which had already adorned the cover of a top fashion magazine. Tre's energy and enthusiasm for life was especially noteworthy since she was born with only partial legs and fingers. When I met Tre I was expecting to discover depression, anger, and unbelief hidden beneath her happy face. I never found it. Instead, **A LIFE THAT MIGHT HAVE BEEN CONSIDERED LESS SIGNIFICANT BY MANY, HAD A HUGE IMPACT UPON ME AND SCORES OF OTHER PEOPLE.**

Most of Tre's impact was due to her faith in God to act like God. She faced her mountain with a faith that was contagious to the faith of others. Instead of focusing on her limitations, she zeroed in on what God could do through her. She gave huge hugs everywhere to everyone, prayed powerfully with people, listened patiently, passed on joy to the downcast, wrote poetry, drew pictures, sang songs, even literally climbed mountains. She wrote to me that she had decided to "live a 'with God' lifestyle and just see how far I can go".

Tre belonged to the Mustard Seed Tribe. She believed in God to multiply the influence of her life and ministry despite her challenges.

CONSIDER THIS: WHEN HAS GOD MOVED A MOUNTAIN FOR YOU?

I've heard hyper-faith preachers take Matthew 17:20 and wave it like a magic wand, promising to send you an actual mustard seed which they have prayed over in order to move your mountain, if you will send them $100 or more. Yet I keep waiting to hear of one actual mountain that has relocated itself due to their mercenary faith.

At the same time, in our critique of the word of faith excesses, I believe **WE ARE IN DANGER OF BELITTLING GOD.** We have succumbed to a scientific rationalism which precludes the supernatural intervention of God. We have tended to slouch toward Nazareth. Matthew 13:58 describes Jesus' ministry in Nazareth this way: "And he did not do many miracles there because of their lack of faith."

The mustard seed is used by Jesus in Matthew 17:20 as a hyperbolic contrast between small and large, from the tiniest common item the Jews knew (the mustard seed) to the most mammoth object they could see (the mountain). The implication was clear—what seems small to you carries disproportionate ability if it is inhabited by the power of God. **YOU DON'T NEED BIG FAITH IF YOUR FAITH IS TRULY IN GOD** instead of yourself or your resources. Even little faith will be big.

CONSIDER THIS: IS YOUR FAITH IN GOD INCREASING? WHAT EVIDENCE ARE YOU USING FOR YOUR ANSWER?

It is this brand of faith which freshly stirs the imagination of disciples to believe for a multiplication of disciples, leaders, ministries and churches. **THIS MUSTARD SEED FAITH REFUSES TO ACCEPT THE STATUS QUO AS THE CEILING FOR THE CHURCH.** It looks at the obstacles holding the advancement of the church back and begins to pray the power of God against the impediments.

The white building on the corner with three dozen faithful saints may look as unlikely as a mustard seed to the community around it. Yet, if this group looks above any of their past disabilities to the ability of God, a whole new future of possibilities is birthed. **FAITH OVERCOMES THE IMPROBABLE.**

Multiplication is sacrificial. It will not happen without risk. **FAITH IS THE FOUNDATION OF RISK-TAKING.**

While Saul and the army of Israel sat around their safe campfires, Jonathan snuck out to see what God might do through faith and action. Jonathan's mustard seed quote from 1 Samuel 14:6 should be tattooed on our hearts – "Nothing can hinder the Lord from saving, whether by many or by few." He was saying since God is God and our trust is in him (and not the size of our army), then let's go move a mountain. Many ministries fail to multiply because their fear of the risk is greater than their faith in God's willingness to act on their behalf.

FAITH

IS THE FOUNDATION OF RISK-TAKING

CONSIDER THIS: WHEN IS THE LAST TIME YOU DID SOMETHING FOR GOD THAT FRIGHTENED YOU?

Four years ago our church was actively planting churches locally and globally. We were doing effective missional work in our own neighborhood through our Light & Life Community Center. Good work for God was going on. We felt like we were still stretching ourselves but the truth was **A DEGREE OF COMPLACENCY HAD CREPT INTO OUR CULTURE.**

At this point, a church building five minutes from our location came up for sale for $1.5 million. Restoring it would cost another $700,000. All this money for a building with a mere 28 parking spots.

The flip side, however, was the historic reality that church buildings in our urban Long Beach setting were nearly nonexistent. It was also true that the Jehovah Witnesses and apartment builders had their eye on the property. Both potential buyers would remove it from true kingdom service. We began to ask the Lord, "Do you want us to acquire this property?"

Honestly, I wasn't personally well-positioned to listen for the Lord's voice. I didn't want to jeopardize the good thing we had going for what seemed a huge risk and a long shot. My fears were clogging my ears. Our Leadership Council and pastors began to earnestly inquire of the Lord. We felt like the Lord was asking in response, "Where's your faith? Is it in me or you?" I was dragging my spiritual feet looking for closed doors, so I wouldn't have to face the mountain.

After much prayer and many admonitions from others with more faith than me, we put in a low offer on the church building, and it was accepted. A month later we closed escrow on a second campus two miles away. Here's where the story is supposed to resolve to the "happily ever after" ending; but that's not the real picture. Honestly we've come through three tough years. There have been moments I wished we'd never purchased the second campus.

But about six months ago momentum began to shift. The mustard seed we had planted began to grow steadily. God did it. Currently over 300 people, almost all new to the church, most from the immediate neighborhood and most previously unchurched, are worshipping in the refurbished sanctuary. **FAITH HAS MULTIPLIED OUR CHURCH.** The mountain moved. Faith has given rise to a whole new branch of the Light & Life river.

Multiplication takes more faith than addition because **MULTIPLICATION REQUIRES GIVING AWAY FROM YOURSELF.** Addition is about gathering; multiplication about releasing. Due to a lack of faith, many pastors, leaders, ministries and churches are trying to win at an inferior game.

When I was in first and second grades, I was king of the chalkboard. For some reason, I could add numbers faster than any other student in my class. The teacher would stand two of us at the board, and we would race to see who could add a column of numbers the fastest. I seldom lost and could stand at the board for half an hour, defeating each new challenger.

But then came third grade and the monster of multiplication. For some reason, I didn't catch on but most of the rest of the class did. By the second half of the year there was a whole new kind of race at the chalkboard, and I was consistently losing. I was better at addition than I had ever been in my life, but now **ADDITION WAS AN INFERIOR GAME TO MULTIPLICATION.**

The church is trying to win at the inferior game of addition. Some of my large church friends may find my language offensive, but honesty compels me to speak reality. The church in North America has been focused on addition with countless seminars on how to grow the church and how to break growth barriers. These are good; they just aren't best. Sometimes good isn't good enough. **SOMETIMES GOOD BECOMES THE DISTRACTION FROM BEST.**

CONSIDER THIS: WHY DO YOU THINK MULTIPLICATION TAKES MORE FAITH THAN ADDITION?

The Pew Research Center's newest report, "America's Changing Religious Landscape," measured the shift in American religion between 2007 and 2014 and their results should sound the alarm for Christian leaders. The report found that **THE PERCENTAGE OF AMERICANS WHO IDENTIFY AS CHRISTIAN HAS DROPPED 8%**, while those who are unaffiliated (which includes atheists, agnostics, and nothing in particular) rose by nearly 7%.[5]

5   Cathy Lynn Grossman, *"Christians lose ground, 'nones' soar in new portrait of US religion,"* Religion News Service, May 12, 2015, http://religionnews.com/2015/05/12/christians-lose-ground-nones-soar-new-portrait-u-s-religion/ (accessed June 8, 2016).

If we keep focusing on trying to win at addition, we will become as irrelevant as I was at my third grade chalkboard. **WE MUST LEARN THE SKILLS OF DISCIPLE-MAKING AND MULTIPLICATION.**

Todd Wilson and Dave Ferguson, founder and president of Exponential, have written a book which is beginning to have a potent effect on the church in America. It is called Becoming a Level Five Multiplying Church and addresses the five conditions of churches.[6]

Level 1 is a church that is experiencing subtraction. It is in decline and seeking to stop the bleeding. This church is in survival mode.

Level 2 is a church that has plateaued. It has been stagnant in addition and multiplication growth. It is seeking to stay even, keep things as they are, preserve the current equilibrium. This church is in status quo mode.

80% OF THE CHURCHES IN AMERICA ARE CURRENTLY IN THESE FIRST TWO LEVELS.

Level 3 is a church that is enjoying addition. It is growing numerically and in other ways. It is seeking to retain as many people as possible. This church is in "church growth" mode.

16% OF CHURCHES ARE ADDING PEOPLE TO THEIR CONGREGATIONS. While we rejoice in this, the question, even in that statistic, is: How much of that is conversion growth instead of Christians moving from existing churches to different churches? We do know a majority of individual church growth is transfer growth.

Level 4 is a church that is reproducing itself by starting new churches. It may or may not be growing in overall numerical or financial ways, but the kingdom is growing because of its sacrifice to begin new congregations. This church is in "church planting" mode.

Less than 4% of churches fit this classification. **96% OF CHURCHES IN AMERICA WILL NEVER START EVEN ONE NEW CHURCH, LET ALONE MULTIPLE CHURCHES.**

Level 5 is a whole different type of church. It is engineered quite distinctly from the other four kinds of churches. Size is not the issue or concern for this church.

6   Todd Wilson and Dave Ferguson, *Becoming a Level Five Multiplying Church Field Guide* (Exponential Resources, 2015).

This is a church that is starting new churches who in turn prioritize launching other new churches. Multiplication is the focus. The goal is not the next church plant but multiple generations of church plants. This church is in the "church movement" mode.

Only a handful of these churches exist in the United States. Churches have not caught this vision. There are many reasons for this dearth of Level Five churches; some of which we will consider in the following chapters.

CONSIDER THIS: WHICH OF THE FIVE LEVELS DO YOU THINK YOUR CHURCH IS AT? WHY?

Regardless of the level your church finds itself in, mustard seed faith is the essential ingredient to move up to the next level God wants for your church or ministry. **FAITH IS WHAT IT TAKES TO RISK TURNING THE VISION INTO ACTION.** Faith is what it takes to stay with the vision through initial resistance.

THE SIZE OF THE CHURCH DOES NOT HAVE TO DEFINE THE IMPACT OF THE CHURCH. A Level 4 or 5 church is not defined by its Sunday morning numerical attendance, or building size, or budget size. Any size of church can choose to form new multiplication DNA.

But it will take mustard seed faith, which looks at the seemingly insignificant reality and sees what God can do. **FAITH SEES THAT GOD CAN SAVE BY MANY OR BY FEW.**

God is looking for those disciples who will dare to believe God to act like God; who will stop letting their fears be bigger than their faith; who will stop majoring in excuses and start exercising courage to try a new way of ministry.

QUESTIONS TO CONSIDER:

1. When has God moved a mountain for you?

2. Is your faith in God increasing? What evidence are using for your answer?

3. When is the last time you did something for God that frightened you?

4. Why do you think multiplication takes more faith than addition?

5. Which of the five levels do you think your church is at? Why?

CHAPTER FOUR: SPICE

WE BELIEVE THE GOSPEL TRANSFORMS CULTURE.

Tab. XII.

MATTHEW 5:13 "You are the salt of the earth. But if the salt loses its saltiness, how can it be made salty again? It is no longer good for anything, except to be thrown out and trampled underfoot."

Salt without saltiness is as good as dirt. Likewise, mustard is one of the most popular spices in the world but not if it has no tanginess. If it loses its mustard-ness it is as spicy as yellow flour. It is the distinct pungent salty/sour/sweet taste that causes us to crave it on every hot dog we eat. **IT'S VALUABLE BECAUSE IT'S DIFFERENT.**

Bruce was one of the best college decathletes in America and a new follower of Jesus. He was raised in a traditional Jewish home but met Jesus personally in college. Bruce wrote a song entitled "Born Again" about the radical change in his life since his Jesus encounter.

As one of Bruce's close friends, I remember his elation when he got his first job. He was most excited about being able to share Jesus with all the folks at work. After his first week I asked Bruce how it was going. He got tears in his eyes, then reported what they had said to him – "Why would we want to be Christians? Christians are just like us. There's no difference. They do the same things we do, talk the same way we do, watch the same shows, chase the same women, drink as much alcohol as we do. The only difference is we don't feel guilty about it and we don't have to get up early on Sundays." Bruce paused and said, "Larry, I didn't know how to respond, so I told them, 'I don't know what to say but watch me for six months and then we will talk.'"

It was a mustard seed challenge.

CONSIDER THIS: HOW OBVIOUS ARE THE DIFFERENCES BETWEEN YOU AND YOUR NON-CHRISTIAN CO-WORKERS, CLASSMATES, NEIGHBORS?

THOSE IN THE MUSTARD SEED TRIBE DON'T WANT TO BLEND IN; they want to stand out. They want the distinction of their lives to speak louder than their words. They want their actions imitated, more than they want their words repeated.

CULTURE IS NOT SOMETHING TO BE CRITIQUED AND CHASTISED with religious speeches. Throwing your religious rules at the culture around you will prove highly ineffective. Instead of saying, "Let ME tell YOU what I believe," how about this: "Watch my life for six

WE DO NOT CHANGE CULTURE

BY CONFORMING TO CULTURE

months and then YOU tell ME what I believe." In other words, "Taste the mustard of my life and tell me whether you'd like to know the ingredients."

CONSIDER THIS: WHAT MIGHT A NON-CHRISTIAN FIND ATTRACTIVE ABOUT THE LIFESTYLE YOU ARE LIVING?

Isn't that what Jesus was saying when, three verses after his declaration about salt losing its flavor, he tells us that **THE ACTIONS OF OUR LIVES MUST BE THE PRIMARY ATTRACTION** to draw people to glorifying God. "In the same way, let your light shine before others, that they may see your good deeds and glorify your Father in heaven" (Matthew 5:16).

Multiplication cannot be a church program to expand the reach of the organization. **MULTIPLICATION MUST FLOW FROM A HEART PASSIONATE TO SEE INDIVIDUALS, NEIGHBORHOODS, CITIES HEALED BY THE POWER OF THE GOSPEL.**

If the gospel loses its potency it loses its power to transform. **WE DO NOT CHANGE CULTURE BY CONFORMING TO CULTURE** in a misdirected effort to relate. We prioritize a humble compassion without compromise. We are distinguished by our servanthood, not our rules. But we do not become like the darkness to bring the light.

CONSIDER THIS: HOW MUCH WOULD YOUR COMMUNITY MISS YOUR CHURCH AND WHY?

We find the brokenness and our hearts are broken by it. From that position of listening, loving, and understanding, we begin to infuse loving actions and spiritual truth into the places of pain. This process begins to actually change the atmosphere in the lives of individuals and neighborhoods. Healing begins to flow.

In the wine country of California, springtime brings a dazzling display of yellow flowers growing between the rows of grapes. These blooms are from the mustard seeds which have been planted as a cover crop in the vineyards. Why mustard? Because mustard can heal the soil in the vineyard.

Mustard serves several healing functions. First, it reduces erosion of the soil. It also adds nitrogen to the soil, improves water penetration, reduces compaction, and improves soil tilth. Most importantly mustard contains high levels of biofumigants. In plain terms, mustard has a pungent odor and sharp taste that damaging, microscopic worms hate. The more mustard, the fewer destructive worms in the soil. Some vineyards have even developed their own strains of mustard plants which are extra spicy to further deter these worms.

This fact can be a powerful reminder of what the gospel is to do in the soil of the communities it enters. It is to heal the soil, to push back the destroying worms in lives and communities. But if it loses its distinctions, its "mustard-ness", it can no longer push back the darkness.

Multiplication needs to always begin with something potent enough and healthy enough that God would want to see it replicated. Cancer multiplies, but not for the good. **MULTIPLYING A RELIGIOUS INSTITUTION OR SICK CHURCH IS NOT GOD'S DESIRE**. The apostle Paul described this brand of "church" as "having a form or shape or outward appearance of godliness but lacking the true power" (2 Timothy 3:5).

If, on the other hand, you have a living organism that has the power to mend broken lives, decrease the darkness, defeat some of Satan's strategies and rescue people for eternity – this is the entity God is yearning to multiply. This is how his heart is expressed to the world.

Three years ago my wife, Dr. Deb Walkemeyer, started the first community garden in Compton, California. If you are unfamiliar with Compton, it is infamous for being the birthplace of hip-hop music and of the Bloods and the Crips (notorious gangs). **EXTREME BROKENNESS, PAIN, AND VIOLENCE STALK THE STREETS OF COMPTON.** Deb's desire was to spread some mustard into a hurting neighborhood.

CONSIDER THIS: HOW DOES YOUR LIFE VISIBLY COMMUNICATE CHRIST'S LOVE IN A PRACTICAL WAY?

Her dissertation for her Doctoral degree was on "Community Gardening as a Means of Transformational Ministry." But she didn't just study the problem and write on it. No, she got her hands dirty. She pulled out a shovel and started digging in the dirt.

Through a series of miracles, **GOD USED A NON-CHRISTIAN CHINESE BUSINESSMAN TO PROVIDE A LARGE PARCEL OF GROUND ON ONE OF THE MOST INFAMOUS STREETS OF COMPTON.** The lot had previously been a one-night stand hotel which had been torn down. The vacant tract then became the place where prostitutes solicited and drug dealers did their deals. It was a border between two of the most violent gangs in Compton. It sat in the middle of an urban food desert, where there were plenty of liquor stores but you had to travel out of the area to buy a real tomato. This Chinese gentleman offered the lot to Deb if she would just grow him a few vegetables every month. Deb and her team prayed over the land and started shoveling.

But they didn't just bring their shovels; they brought their love, their hugs, their ears to listen, their hands to serve and their hearts to heal. Their vision was that this piece of land could bloom like a rose in the desert and become a place of shalom, God's peace.

They started inviting ex-felons, prostitutes, dealers, homeless folks, gang members to work in the garden—and they came. 70 garden beds were planted, and as the vegetables began to grow so did the relationships. Although Deb, as a sixty-year-old white lady (a rarity in Compton) had to fight the misconceptions that she was a popo (Police), a narc (Narcotics agent) or an immigration officer; her love began to bridge the divide. Bob, the co-leader and a minister with the Navigators, had been planting good seeds in the community for years and they began to sprout.

Slowly the neighborhood began to change. The soil began to heal. The darkness was pushed back. A documentary movie was made that featured the garden. The Executive Producer was Academy Award winner John Legend, who also wrote music for the movie. The chaos in the neighborhood began to calm, and the garden became a refuge, a place of shalom.

In the middle of the garden is a pergola with grapes growing over the top of it, flowers around the base of it, and benches to sit on. A fountain is in the middle. One of the prostitutes who is trying to escape the lifestyle told us, "I just come here to sit and think because it's the only place I really feel peace." One of the Hollywood producers said, "There's something special about this place. It's like an island of peace." They are experiencing the shalom of God.

They are tasting the mustard.

Sex trafficking, gang violence, and criminal activity have decreased in that immediate vicinity since the beauty of God's love has moved into the neighborhood. The Compton Mayor and the Congresswoman for the area have lauded the garden for its work. Best of all, some of those working in the garden have made decisions for Christ and are now active in local churches, including ours.

The ministry of the garden, however, is not just what's happening in the particular place. It is what is occurring through the garden. **THE GARDEN IS MULTIPLYING.** Deb and her team are raising up other gardeners. Our group has now been asked to put gardens in all the schools of Compton and help bring the same kind of shalom to school communities.

CONSIDER THIS: WHERE IS AN AREA OF BROKENNESS IN YOUR COMMUNITY THAT YOU COULD BRING GOD'S SHALOM (PEACE) OR HEALING TO?

Sadly, Compton has hundreds of churches but the locals will tell you they "hide behind their walls and expect everyone to come to them". **THE SALT IS THERE BUT IT'S STUCK IN THE SALT SHAKER.**

Have you ever had a meal that really needed salt but when you went to shake the shaker, the salt was clogged up on the inside? It didn't want to leave the shaker and do what it was created to do. It just wanted to stay safe with the rest of the salt.

If your church went out of business, how long would it take the community to notice? How many neighbors would be really sad that it shut down? How many lives in the area would be different because you weren't there anymore? **IF YOUR CHURCH IS BEING SALT AND MUSTARD IN THE COMMUNITY, IT WILL LEAVE A BIG HOLE IF IT'S UPROOTED.**

Jesus prayed for this kind of impact in John 17:15-18: "My prayer is not that you take them out of the world but that you protect them from the evil one. They are not of the world, even as I am not of it. Sanctify them by the truth; your word is truth. As you sent me into the world, I have sent them into the world."

A paraphrase of Jesus' words might say, "Don't let my people stay stuck in the salt shaker, huddled up inside their church buildings. But don't let them become like the world either. **MAKE THEM DISTINCT BECAUSE THEY ACTUALLY LIVE BY YOUR WORD.** Send them into the world so they can impact it with love and truth in the same way I did".

A boat is not fulfilling its design unless it gets in the water. If it sits in the garage it looks like a boat, but it's not acting like a boat. But if you put the boat in the water, and the water gets in the boat, the boat is going to sink. The boat must be in the water without the water being in the boat. Similarly, **THE CHURCH MUST GO INTO THE WORLD WITHOUT LETTING THE WORLD CHANGE THE CHURCH.**

This is the kind of church we need to see multiplied across America. One that gets its hands dirty with pain and darkness without allowing the dirt to live under its fingernails. This is a mustard seed kind of church.

The church must be missional or we will be multiplying institutionalism instead of redemption. These **LIFESTYLES OF HOLINESS AND ACTS OF LOVE WILL HEAL NEIGHBORHOODS** and awaken hearts to Jesus. I've seen it and God declares it in 1 Peter 2:12 "Live such good lives among the pagans that, though they accuse you of doing wrong, they may see your good deeds and glorify God on the day he visits us."

QUESTIONS TO CONSIDER:

1. How obvious are the differences between you and your non-Christian co-workers, classmates, neighbors?

2. What might a non-Christian find attractive about the lifestyle you are living?

3. How much would your community miss your church and why?

4. How does your life visibly communicate Christ's love in a practical way?

5. Where is an area of brokenness in your community that you could bring God's shalom (peace) or healing to?

CHAPTER FIVE: FIELD

WE BELIEVE KINGDOM PEOPLE ARE TO BE PLANTED IN THE WORLD.

> **MATTHEW 13:31, 38** "He told them another parable: 'The kingdom of heaven is like a mustard seed, which a man took and planted in his field. The field is the world, and the good seed stands for the people of the kingdom. The weeds are the people of the evil one.'"

I remember the first time I heard the term "mission field." I was maybe five years of age. I already knew what a baseball field, an air field and a wheat field were. Later I would learn of the battle field, the medical field and eventually, the force field.

Different images came to my mind when my mom informed me we were going to visit my uncle who was working in the "mission field" in Africa. Perhaps it was like a farm and he was growing things. Or maybe it was a like a big grassy meadow and he was building houses there. Or was it like a field of strawberries and he was picking strawberries?

Consequently, I started quizzing my mother to try and form a more accurate picture of this type of field. She patiently explained that my uncle lived in a small house among the African people, and everyday he was trying to love them, serve them, and teach them skills, but most importantly he was seeking to tell them about Jesus. I didn't know what that had to do with a field, but it sounded cool to me and I wanted to go see this mission field.

CONSIDER THIS: CAN YOU NAME YOUR PRIMARY "HARVEST FIELDS," THE PLACES YOU INTERACT MOST FREQUENTLY OR DEEPLY WITH NON-CHRISTIANS?

In Matthew 13, Jesus had just told a story about a farmer who planted good wheat seed but then was attacked by an enemy who snuck into his field and scattered weed seed. Listen to Jesus' explanation about who the characters in the story are:

"He answered, '**THE ONE WHO SOWED THE GOOD SEED IS THE SON OF MAN**. The field is the world, and the good seed stands for the people of the kingdom. The weeds are the people of the evil one, and the enemy who sows them is the devil. The harvest is the end of the age, and the harvesters are angels" (Matthew 13:37-39).

You rarely hear this story explained accurately. The sower is the Son of Man. The seed is the people of the kingdom. It is us – those who have the true seed of Christ living in them. **WE BECOME THE SEED THAT CAN BRING LIFE**. But in order for this harvest to be created, we must be planted in the world and live among the weeds—people not of the kingdom. The field is our calling, our temporary residence, our mission.

I believe we need to read John 1:14 next to this Jesus story to fully understand it. "The Word became flesh and made his dwelling among us. We have seen his glory, the glory of the one and only Son, who came from the Father, full of grace and truth." Or as Petersen poignantly paraphrases the first phrase – "The Word became flesh and blood, and moved into the neighborhood…" **JESUS WENT TO THE FIELD.**

The Mustard Seed Tribe asks God to plant them in the field of the world. They look for those places where their lives intersect with the world and ask, **"HOW CAN I PLANT MY INFLUENCE FOR THE KINGDOM IN THIS FIELD?"**

Multiplication is not a church program to increase our market share. **MULTIPLICATION IS AN URGENT RESCUE MISSION UNDERTAKEN ON THE TURF OF THE WORLD FOR THE SAKE OF THE LOST.** Multiplication movements are incarnational and evangelistic. Movements don't preach to the choir; they reach to the margins. They innovate and infiltrate to influence the world, just like John Wesley taught us.

On March 31, 1739 John Wesley penned the following words in his journal: "In the evening I reached Bristol and met Mr. Whitefield there. I could scarcely reconcile myself at first to this strange way of preaching in the fields, of which he set me an example on Sunday; I had been all my life (till very lately) so tenacious of every point relating to decency and order that I should have thought the saving of souls almost a sin if it had not been done in a church."[7]

Wesley had thought "saving of souls" was work to be done in the church not in the field. He was a conservative high church man. He felt people should come to church to hear the gospel. But the Spirit of God used George Whitefield to convince him otherwise; that the seed needed to be planted in the fields.

Preaching in the field would stretch Wesley far outside his comfort zone. It would humble him. On April 2, 1739 he recorded in his journal, "At four in the afternoon, I submitted to be more vile and proclaimed in the highways the glad tidings of salvation, speaking from a little eminence in a ground adjoining to the city, to about three thousand people."[8]

7   John Wesley, "Wesley Begins Field-preaching," Journal of John Wesley, Christian Classics Ethereal Library, http://www.ccel.org/ccel/wesley/journal.vi.iii.i.html (accessed July 1, 2016).
8   Ibid.

Two months later he would compose some of his most famous words: "I look upon all the world as my parish; thus far I mean, that in whatever part of it I am, I judge it meet, right, and my bounden duty to declare unto all that are willing to hear, the glad tidings of salvation." –Journal, June 11, 1739.[9]

The world was his field. His right and duty was to declare to anyone willing to hear the good news of Jesus...regardless of location. This change of venue would be a distinguishing mark of his ministry. He realized open-air service was effective in reaching those who would not enter most churches. For the next fifty years **WESLEY PREACHED WHEREVER HE COULD ASSEMBLE PEOPLE**, even using his father's tombstone at Epworth as a pulpit on more than one occasion, preaching life in the field of the dead.[10]

Wesley's new conviction and practice was multiplied among his followers and soon preaching in the fields was common among the Methodist leaders. It was this multiplication of lay preachers entering the world to proclaim the good news that led to the dramatic spread of the movement.

CONSIDER THIS: ARE THERE PLACES YOU DON'T DESIRE TO SHARE THE GOSPEL BUT MAY BE FRUITFUL IF YOU DID, LIKE WESLEY'S OPEN-AIR PREACHING?

Today in America open field preaching is not an effective means of reaching the lost. Nevertheless, there is a principle in it which is largely absent from the American church and is blocking the movement we seek. People of the kingdom have focused on serving in the church instead of serving on the mission field. **THE BUSYNESS OF RUNNING THE CHURCH PROGRAM PREVENTS THE MISSIONARIES FROM REACHING INTO THE FIELD.**

Not being first century Jewish gardeners causes us to miss the unsuspected irony in the words of Jesus when he illustrated the kingdom this way in Luke 13:19: "It is like a mustard seed, which a man took and planted in his garden..." Jewish gardeners might have responded with shock and dismay to that first line of the story asking, "WHY? Why would a good Jewish farmer do that?"

You must understand at this time mustard seed was not legal to plant in your garden. Why? Because the mustard would not stay in its own row. It would not just isolate

9   James Pedlar, "Four John Wesley Quotes Everyone Should Know," May 21, 2011, https://jamespedlar.wordpress.com/2011/05/21/four-john-wesley-quotes-everyone-should-know/ (accessed July 1, 2016).
10   "John Wesley," Wikipedia, https://en.wikipedia.org/wiki/John_Wesley (accessed July 1, 2016).

TOO OFTEN WE OFFER TO GOD OUR SUNDAY LIFE

INSTEAD OF OUR EVERYDAY LIFE

itself in the neat and orderly place it was assigned in the garden. Instead it would bust out of its row and begin to dangerously mingle with the other plants.

So when the first century listeners heard Jesus call his kingdom a mustard seed that grows rapidly, they felt an inner conflict. Was this a divine blessing or a violation? Is this good or bad? Is it clean or unclean? But Jesus clearly meant this word picture to be applauded. Why? Jesus loves it when his kingdom gets out of its religious box and begins to mingle with the world around it.

I've walked into churches and seen the straight rows of pews with their straight backs filled with straight people and thought, "Ah, a nice religious garden, but where's the mustard? Where's the mingling, the engagement with the world? Where's the kingdom breaking out of the row assigned to it? Where's the mustard reaching out to the lost?"

The theology of Evangelical Christians is not universalism. Universalism is the belief that eventually all will be saved, rendering evangelism as ultimately inconsequential. Yet, **MOST EVANGELICAL CHRISTIANS ARE FUNCTIONAL UNIVERSALISTS.** To prove this simply ask them the following four questions –
1. Do you know the names of your neighbors on your street?
2. Do you know if they know Jesus as their Savior?
3. Are you praying for them regularly by name?
4. What is your plan to reach them with the good news?

When Christians share with me the belief that God is calling them into career ministry here or abroad my first question is **"WHAT ARE YOU DOING TO REACH YOUR NEIGHBORS NOW?"** The idea that God would send you to a mission field half way around the world when you won't walk to the mission field next door is deception.

CONSIDER THIS: DO YOU SEE UNIVERSALISM AT WORK IN THE WORLD AROUND YOU? HOW CONVINCED ARE YOU THAT JOHN 14:6 IS ABSOLUTELY TRUE FOR EVERYONE?

When I arrived in Africa and saw my uncle's mission field, it was very different than my young mind imagined. It was a mechanic's shop. His days consisted of fixing the broken parts of bicycles, automobiles, windmills, and wheelbarrows. As he brought healing to busted axels he was talking to the Africans about the healer named Jesus.

At nights he was having Bible studies in his home, and on weekends he was leading a new church for those who were responding to Jesus. He wasn't staying in his church box; he was mingling with the locals on their turf.

But my uncle was not just a mechanic; he was a multiplier. He was training young men to become Christian mechanics. These men were mechanics with a message. Their passion was to be excellent mechanics, but even more so to be evangelistic Christians. My uncle was being seed in the field and sending more seed into the field.

WHERE IS YOUR FIELD? It is wherever your daily life intersects with people who don't know Jesus. God desires to plant you there into the lives of people. It is your love and service in your daily encounters that open the door for the gospel. I tell our church, "Love people so deeply, practically and consistently that they are forced to ask, 'Why?' Live so your life demands an explanation."

CONSIDER THIS: RETAKE THE FOUR QUESTIONS OF THE NEIGHBOR TEST ABOVE AND ASK YOURSELF, WHAT FEAR, LIE, OR EXCUSE IS KEEPING ME FROM DOING BETTER ON THIS TEST?

The Message paraphrases Romans 12:1 "So here's what I want you to do, God helping you: Take your everyday, ordinary life—your sleeping, eating, going-to-work, and walking-around life—and place it before God as an offering." **TOO OFTEN WE OFFER TO GOD OUR SUNDAY LIFE INSTEAD OF OUR EVERYDAY LIFE.**

There are too few missionaries, meaning Christians living on a daily mission. This statement is not just based on research or experience, although I could offer statistics as proof. It is based on the words of Jesus in Luke 10:2: "He told them, 'The harvest is plentiful, but the workers are few. Ask the Lord of the harvest, therefore, to send out workers into his harvest field.'"

HOW DO WE MOVE INTO OUR MISSION FIELD?

1. **WE PRAY FOR OUR NEIGHBORS**, co-workers, classmates, golf buddies, etc. by name.

When we care enough to call out names to the Lord on a regular basis we will likely see more impact from our efforts.

2. **WE DO EXCELLENT WORK AT OUR WORK.**

Whatever field of work we are in, we do good work in that field.

One of my favorite Martin Luther King, Jr. quotes says, "If a man is called to be a streetsweeper, he should sweep streets even as Michelangelo painted, or Beethoven composed music, or Shakespeare wrote poetry. He should sweep streets so well that all the hosts of heaven and earth will pause to say, here lived a great streetsweeper who did his job well."[11]

3. **WE AUTHENTICALLY LOVE PEOPLE** and look for opportunities to serve.

There is one thing you can know about every person you work with: they want to be loved. Love works. People desire love, but we must look to love them in ways that are meaningful to them. Find the point of need they have and seek to serve them in it.

4. **WE BUILD REDEMPTIVE FRIENDSHIPS.**

It is hard to have a high impact on people from a distance. Friendships bring us together in ways that open the doors of the heart.

Someone once challenged me with this question: "If you want someone to make heaven their home, are you willing to share your home with them?" Having friends over for food was the way Levi reached out to his friends (Mark 2:14-17). It's still a good idea today.

5. **WE LOOK FOR OPENINGS TO OPEN OUR MOUTHS.**

Opening your heart and your life is not adequate. There comes a moment when you need to open your mouth to share the truth of the gospel. As one who is urgent about your friend's salvation you are looking diligently for those opportunities. You understand Romans 10:17: "Consequently, faith comes from hearing the message, and the message is heard through the word about Christ."

11   Sharon Sequeira, *MLK Quote of the Week*, The King Center, April 9, 2013, http://www. thekingcenter.org/blog/mlk-quote-week-all-labor-uplifts-humanity-has-dignity-and-importance-and-should-be-undertaken (accessed July 1, 2016).

CONSIDER THIS: HAVE YOU EVER TAUGHT SOMEONE ELSE HOW TO SHARE THE GOSPEL? CAN THAT BE A SPIRITUAL GOAL FOR YOU THIS YEAR?

MUSTARD SEED DOES NOT GROW WHEN PLANTED ON A CHURCH PEW. It must be planted in the field. Our goal is not Sunday School awards for Bible memory verses, but souls finding new life through the Word. We can't multiply ministry without reaching the lost in the field.

QUESTIONS TO CONSIDER:

1. Can you name your primary "harvest fields," the places you interact most frequently or deeply with non-Christians?

2. Are there places you don't desire to share the gospel but may be fruitful if you did, like Wesley's open-air preaching?

3. Do you see universalism at work in the world around you? How convinced are you that John 14:6 is absolutely true for everyone?

4. Retake the four questions of the neighbor test above and ask yourself, "What fear, lie, or excuse is keeping me from doing better on this test?"

5. Have you ever taught someone else how to share the gospel? Can that be a spiritual goal for you this year?

CHAPTER SIX:
FlOWERS

WE BELIEVE TRAINING CROSS-BEARING DISCIPLES IS THE LIFE OF MULTIPLICATION

LUKE 9:23: "Then he said to them all: 'Whoever wants to be my disciple must deny themselves and take up their cross daily and follow me.'"

I watched a video recently in which ISIS crucified five men. It was an ugly scene which left me shaken by the shocking torture of it all. As I reflected on the injustice and pain of it, I was hit with the realization that what I had just witnessed was far tamer than the crucifixion of Jesus.

Consequently, to speak of the beauty of the cross seems illogical, irreverent, and preposterous. The transformation of an implement of torture to a treasured piece of jewelry seems the height of paradox. Only the resurrection could unleash such a powerful reversal. Without the victory of Jesus over death, the cross would not only be the ultimate torture, it would symbolize utter defeat.

Jesus' death, however, is good news forever because the cross did not have the final word. It has an irreducible splendor because it pictures the pinnacle of God's love for us. It becomes our life compass, pointing to the truest north. **THE CROSS NOT ONLY SAVES US FROM OUR PAST, IT DIRECTS US TO OUR FUTURE.** It becomes the message of our lives.

The apostle Paul writes, "For the message of the cross is foolishness to those who are perishing, but to us who are being saved it is the power of God." (1 Corinthians 1:18) He highlights that one of the most visible demarcations between the perishing and the living is their view of the cross. For the first group it is nothing but ugly foolishness. To the second group **THE CROSS IS THE EXQUISITE WISDOM OF GOD.**

CONSIDER THIS: WHAT BEAUTIES OR VIRTUES HAVE YOU SEEN DEVELOP IN YOUR LIFE AS A RESULT OF EMBRACING THE CROSS?

John Wesley, in his instructions to his preachers regarding what to preach, states, "Let us strongly insist upon inward and outward holiness; and, with this view, set forth Christ as evidently crucified before their eyes; Christ in all the riches of his grace, justifying us by his blood, and sanctifying us by his Spirit...Choose the plainest texts you can."[12]

---

12   Chris Ritter, "*John Wesley's Seven Tips on Sermon Content*," People Need Jesus, July 15, 2015, https://peopleneedjesus.net/2015/07/15/john-wesleys-seven-tips-on-sermon-content/ (accessed June 13, 2016).

Wesley was impressing the messengers of the gospel to **MAKE THE CROSS CENTRAL AND KEEP IT PLAIN.** There is a splendid glory and power when the simplicity of the cross is allowed to rise above the murmur of the theological debates in which we are so easily embroiled.

One of the remarkable features of the mustard plant is the shape of its attractive bright yellow flowers. Mustard belongs to the flowering plant family Brassicaceae, also known as the crucifers. Cruciferae is an older name for the family. It means "cross-bearing," because **THE FOUR PETALS OF THE FLOWERS ARE REMINISCENT OF A CROSS.**

When Jesus told us his kingdom is like a mustard plant, he had selected a plant with a blossom that told a story—in the center of its beauty was the cross. It is this cross-shaped flower that attracts the bees that pollinate the flowers. Once pollinated, the yellow blossoms become seedpods containing hundreds of seeds which multiply the species. **FROM THE CROSS SPRINGS LIFE AND OFFSPRING, AND THE KINGDOM EXPANDS.**

It is the centrality of the cross that creates a life of beauty in the believer. The cross is shorthand for the gospel story. When a person has embraced the cross as their salvation, as their hope of heaven, as the declaration of their personal value, as the definition of their true identity, as their security for eternity; then an inimitable attractiveness and fragrance is released through their life to the world.

The cross is the one-time event our salvation flows from, and it is the daily surrender of our lives to Christ. We live because of the cross, and **WE LIVE TO BROADCAST THE POWER OF THE CROSS.** This requires us taking up our own cross every day.

In high school I was a star football player (think big fish, small pond). In our rural part of Kansas, football was a big deal and being the team captain was a dream for the elementary school children of our town. Consequently, after football games I would be deluged with fourth and fifth graders wanting my autograph. I always signed my name and then added, "Galatians 2:20," hoping they would go home, find a Bible, and look up my life verse.

Galatians 2:20 always seemed to me to be Paul's life verse: "I have been crucified with Christ; and it is no longer I who live, but Christ lives in me; and the life which I now live in the flesh I live by faith in the Son of God, who loved me and gave Himself up for me."

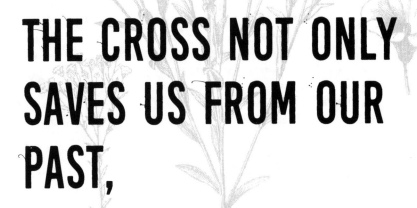

THE CROSS NOT ONLY SAVES US FROM OUR PAST,

IT DIRECTS US TO OUR FUTURE

CONSIDER THIS: WHAT HAVE YOU HAD TO DIE TO BECAUSE OF YOUR PRIORITY UPON THE CROSS OF JESUS?

In one glorious verse Paul gathers up the truths of God's love, Christ's sacrifice, our response by faith, and the power of Christ living in us. This verse stands as a central truth for believers, ministries and churches who hope to multiply.

THE MUSTARD SEED TRIBE CONSISTS OF DISCIPLES WHO HAVE BELIEVED UPON THE POWER OF THE CROSS and dedicated their lives to imprinting its DNA into the lives of other disciples.

The mustard flower is beautiful, but it must also produce seeds—offspring—who will propagate to create the next generation. It must give birth to seeds which will grow into flowers which also have the cross at the center. The mustard plant must drive its DNA deep enough into the seeds it produces that the cross will never be lost. We are thousands of generations from the first mustard plant, yet **EVERY YELLOW MUSTARD FLOWER STILL HAS THE CROSS IN THE MIDDLE.**

The cross and multiplication cannot be separated, but the church seems to try. Churches are full of doers but not disciplers; people who want to pray but not teach others to pray, who want to pass out bulletins but don't want to pass on the DNA of disciple-making, who want to minister but not to multiply. **THE AVERAGE CHRISTIAN HAS NO APPRENTICE IN CHRIST.**

After a distinguished performing career, virtuoso violinist Jascha Heifetz accepted an appointment as professor of music at UCLA. Asked what had prompted his change of career, Heifetz replied: "Violin playing is a perishable art. It must be passed on as a personal skill; otherwise it is lost."[13]

When Paul was writing to Pastor Timothy about how to move the gospel movement forward he gave very clear instructions. He told Timothy how to proceed and how to protect the DNA of the kingdom. "And the things you have heard me say in the presence of many witnesses entrust to reliable people who will also be qualified to teach others" (2 Timothy 2:2).

---

13   "A Perishable Art," Today in the Word, February 8, 1997, accessed on Bible.org, https://bible.org/illustration/perishable-art, (accessed June 13, 2016).

This verse may be the magna carta for multiplication. If I were forced to select one verse from the Bible to base the methodology of the mission on, I would choose this verse. It is a description of what the early church did to cause the gospel to spread like wildfire.

2 Timothy 2:2 describes what Paul was doing and what he was training his disciples to do. It is also a verse picturing how the disciples were carrying out the last command of Jesus when he told them to go to all the world and make disciples, baptizing them and teaching them to follow his teachings (Matthew 28:19,20). Paul was passing the cross forward.

2 Timothy 2:2 also describes what Jesus had done with his own disciples. When Jesus called them he was simple and clear about his mission and the method he would use to accomplish it. "'Come, follow me,' Jesus said, 'and I will send you out to fish for people'" (Matthew 4:19). **JESUS WAS DECLARING THAT HIS MISSION WAS TO REACH PEOPLE.** He method was to teach disciples to imitate him, to learn what he taught and how he lived.

As has often been noted, there are four generations represented in 2 Timothy 2:2. Paul to Timothy is the first generation. Timothy to "reliable people" is generation two. Reliable people to those "qualified to teach" is the third generation. These teachers to "others" is the fourth generation. Paul was calling for "4G" multiplication.

CONSIDER THIS: 2 TIMOTHY 2:2 IS THE PIVOTAL VERSE FOR MULTIPLICATION. WHO DISCIPLED YOU? WHO IS YOUR PAUL, AND WHO IS YOUR DISCIPLE?

Dawson Trotman, the founder of the Navigators ministry, was one of the most effective disciple-makers in history. One of his descriptions of disciple-making is undoubtedly a key reason for such fruitfulness. Trotman said, **"YOU HAVEN'T MADE A DISCIPLE UNTIL YOUR DISCIPLE MAKES A DISCIPLE."**[14]

This definition of disciple-making places the emphasis on the most crucial element in disciple-making: the transference of DNA that will multiply. Your disciple may know a lot of theology, they may have changed every sinful habit they have, they may serve in the soup kitchen and crisis pregnancy clinic, they may witness at work, but the big question is, will they reproduce themselves? Will they plant the centrality of the cross

---

14   Quoted by Todd Wilson, founder of Exponential, Miami, FL, February 10, 2016.

deeply enough in the life of another disciple that the generational chain will not be broken?" Redefining discipleship in terms of reproduction is a game-changer.

In most of the animal kingdom, **MATURITY IS EVIDENCED NOT BY HOW BIG OR OLD AN ANIMAL IS, BUT BY THE AGE AT WHICH THE ANIMAL CAN REPRODUCE.** As Westerners we balk at the thought that Mary was less than 16 years of age when she gave birth to Jesus, yet she had reached a level of physiological maturity. She undoubtedly had more growing up to do and would mature emotionally and spiritually in the days ahead, but she was capable of reproduction.

For too long our working priorities in disciple-making have been to teach them more, help them sin less, and motivate them to work harder in the church. We have failed to emphasize the most important skill—Can they make another disciple? Are they passionate to do so?

This is where the willingness to bear the cross comes in. Cross-bearing is not carrying the troubles that come your way in life. **CROSS-BEARING IS A DAILY SURRENDER OF YOUR LIFE FOR CHRIST.** Just as Adam laid down his life and Eve came forth; just as Christ laid down his life and the church came forth; so disciples lay down their lives and new disciples are birthed.

CONSIDER THIS: WHAT DOES IT MEAN TO YOU PERSONALLY TO CARRY YOUR CROSS DAILY?

MULTIPLICATION MOVEMENTS ALWAYS BEGIN AT THE INDIVIDUAL LEVEL. While planting new churches is the desired endgame, you won't see that achieved on a consistent basis unless you teach multiplication of individual disciples. The church is a gathering of disciples, and if individual disciples believe in multiplication, then it's a natural step for churches to practice it as well. Disciples who reproduce themselves in other disciples want to see their church reproduce into other churches.

I was recently thinking about a popular saying I love: "If you give a man a fish, you feed him for a day. If you teach a man to fish, you feed him for life." The saying doesn't go far enough to solve the hunger problem in the world. It needs a subsequent phrase that reads, "If you teach a man to teach others to fish, you feed a village forever." When everyone is fishing but also, even more importantly, raising up other fishermen and women, a movement has begun.

CONSIDER THIS: THE CROSS GIVES US LIFE AND CALLS US TO DIE. SHOULD DISCIPLE-MAKING BE BASED ON OUR FEELINGS, DESIRES, GIFTS AND DISCRETIONARY TIME, OR SHOULD IT BE A DISCIPLINED PRIORITY IN OUR LIVES?

THE POWER OF THE CROSS IS THE PRIMARY DNA WE MUST IMPART TO OUR DISCIPLES. We must embed that DNA so deeply in them that when they reproduce spiritual offspring that priority is just as beautiful and clear in the third, the fourth, and all ensuing generations.

We must also help our disciples to understand that the call of the cross is to lay down their own lives so they can duplicate their life of faith in someone else who will repeat the process. **THE CROSS GIVES US LIFE, BUT IT ALSO CALLS US TO DIE TO OURSELVES SO WE CAN BRING LIFE TO OTHERS.** Mustard flowers die in order to produce mustard plant seeds. This is the beauty for which God is looking.

QUESTIONS TO CONSIDER:

1. What beauties or virtues have you seen develop in your life as a result of embracing the cross?

2. What have you had to die to because of your priority upon the cross of Jesus?

3. 2 Timothy 2:2 is the pivotal verse for multiplication. Who discipled you? Who is your Paul, and who is your disciple?

4. What does it mean to you personally to carry your cross daily?

5. The cross give us life and calls us to die. Should disciple-making be based on our feelings, desires, gifts and discretionary time, or should it be a disciplined priority in our lives?

CHAPTER SEVEN: BIRDS

WE BELIEVE GOD EMPOWERS UNLIKELY PEOPLE TO UNCOMMON MINISTRY IN UNEXPECTED PLACES.

MATTHEW 13:3,32 "He told them another parable: 'The kingdom of heaven is like a mustard seed, which a man took and planted in his field. Though it is the smallest of all seeds, yet when it grows, it is the largest of garden plants and becomes a tree, so that the birds come and perch in its branches.'"

Birds weren't welcome in the well-ordered gardens of the first century Israelis. The branches of the mustard plant gave these birds shelter, a place to rest and thrive, even a place to call home. These small, common birds which perched there became a vital part of the rapid spread of the mustard plant.

My friend, Brian Bolt, met Christ in the back of an ambulance after being shot point blank in the face for a drug deal gone bad.

On March 17, 2002 Brian was hanging out and drinking with friends at the Melody Manner Bar in Barrelville, Maryland. He was 23 and a profitable drug dealer. Sometime during the evening a disgruntled drug customer pulled a .22 caliber pistol out, pointed it at Brian's face and pulled the trigger. Brian told me, "All I could see was blood pouring out like water coming out of a spigot". Brian was left there to die and that's what he wanted.

The ambulance arrived, and on the trip to the hospital the E.M.T. told Brian his condition was serious and then asked the question, "Do you know Christ as your personal savior?" Through the pain Brian grunted "no" and the E.M.T. prayed a salvation prayer over him. Brian felt a peace come over him as he agreed with the prayer and then lost consciousness.

When Brian finally regained awareness, he was informed he would have severe permanent brain damage. He was paralyzed on the left side, his jaw was shattered, and the bullet was lodged in his carotid artery. After 75 days he regained most of his movement on the left side and began to speak again. At last he was sent home to finish recovering.

Brian remembered what had happened in the back of the ambulance but he didn't understand it. He was soon back on the streets doing and dealing drugs. But, not long after his release, he was walking the street when two common-looking men walked up to him and said, "God has a message for you. God has a purpose for you. Come with us and we will bring you into a men's recovery home. You can stay here and live with us; you don't need to live on the streets anymore. **WE BELIEVE THAT GOD**

GOD EMPOWERS UNLIKELY PEOPLE

TO UNCOMMON MINISTRY

IN UNEXPECTED PLACES.

HAS A CALL ON YOUR LIFE.[15] Brian went to live at the Christian Recovery Home in Los Angeles.

Eventually, Brian ended up at Allison Park Church in Pittsburgh, PA. One day, having lunch with his pastor Jeff Leake, Brian said, "I want to plant a church." Pastor Jeff, an ardent believer in the Spirit's ability to use unlikely people responded, "Let's do it!"

CONSIDER THIS: WHAT LEVEL OF SKILLS AND TRAINING WOULD A PERSON NEED TO LEAD IN YOUR CURRENT MODEL OF CHURCH?

A great adventure was birthed that day, a multiplication example that exceeds almost all contemporary examples in the United States. Brian not only planted a church, but he planted a network of church planting called CityReach. As of this writing **56 CHURCHES HAVE BEEN PLANTED AND 30 ARE IN THE WORKS FOR THIS YEAR.**

How have they done it? In my opinion their "secret sauce" is revealed in their mission statement – "CITYREACH NETWORK plants and develops LIFE-GIVING CHURCHES by using unlikely people in overlooked places for extraordinary things."[16] **BRIAN'S OWN STORY IS FILLED WITH NORMAL PEOPLE WHO WERE WILLING TO TAKE THE MISSION OF JESUS INTO DAILY, YET UNCOMMON PLACES.**

"Birds in mustard branches" is how I see the success of CityReach. These are ordinary people believing that, with God, they can do the unexpected. Different scholars see various meanings in the birds and the branches in Jesus' parable. One thing is certain: birds were not welcome in Palestinian gardens. To this day, all the countries I travel to have one thing in common in their private agriculture – some strategy to keep the birds out.

The field in this story, however, is unique. The sower actually intentionally plants a tiny but notorious mustard seed in his field. He watches this seed grow into a wide and tall bush until it is perhaps 10 to 14 feet tall. The farmer seems to delight in watching the birds come and find their place on the welcoming branches.

What is not in view in the parable, but is vitally true in nature, is that these common birds serve a great purpose. There is a symbiotic relationship between the birds and the mustard plant. As the birds are embraced by the branches, the seeds of the

15 *"From Drug Dealer to Church Planter: Brian Bolt,"* PennDel Ministry Network, May 2, 2014, https://penndel.org/tag/lead-pastor (accessed June 16, 2016).
16 City Reach Network, http://cityreachnetwork.org/what-we-do/ (accessed June 16, 2016).

mustard plant stick to their feet and wings. Once the birds fly off the branch, the seeds begin to fall off their feathers and land in fresh territory where the mustard plant has not yet propagated. These unremarkable birds become profound planters of mustard plants in new untouched areas.

The Mustard Seed Tribe believes **GOD EMPOWERS UNLIKELY PEOPLE TO UNCOMMON MINISTRY IN UNEXPECTED PLACES** for the sake of the multiplication of his kingdom.

Philip, the evangelist, is my model for "ordinary" disciples. He wasn't one of the 12 apostles. In fact, he's not even mentioned until Acts 6 when there is an election for "table waiters" to help out the widows. Philip is nominated as one full of the Spirit and wisdom. He was willing to serve and began his ministry as an administrator and caregiver. But Philip was destined for more. His heart was to see the lost meet Jesus and to see the church multiply. He believed the Holy Spirit would use him, and over the next pages of Acts we see a deliverance ministry, a healing ministry, an evangelistic ministry, and a missionary ministry flow out of Philip's surrender. He also multiplied himself, partly by raising four daughters who practiced the ministry of the Word.

CONSIDER THIS: HAVE YOU SEEN GOD USE AN UNLIKELY PERSON IN UNEXPECTED WAYS?

Scripture tells us that the Holy Spirit desires to take ordinary believers to a whole new level of impact. If pastors were honest, too often their vision for church members is to see them pass out bulletins, bake cookies, collect the offering, attend church workdays, and perhaps serve on the church finance board. But **GOD BUILT EVERY BELIEVER TO CHANGE THE WORLD.** Limiting believers is like keeping a racing boat in a park pond.

WE WERE SAVED FOR MORE THAN GIVING KIDDY RIDES.

In the Reformation, Martin Luther constantly used 1 Peter 2:9—"... you are royal priests ..." —as a key truth explaining, "In this way we are all priests, as many of us as are Christians."

When Luther referred to the priesthood of all believers, he was maintaining that the plowboy and the milkmaid could do priestly work. In fact, their plowing and milking was priestly work. So there was no hierarchy where the priesthood was a vocation and milking the cow was not. Both were tasks that God called his followers to do, each according to their gifts.[17]

CONSIDER THIS: WHAT KIND OF POSITIONS ARE MOST VOLUNTEERS RECRUITED FOR?

We must introduce people to Christ and to their true vocation—priesthood. **WHEN YOUR PARADIGM CHANGES TO MULTIPLICATION, THE PRIESTS GET TO DO PRIESTLY STUFF.** They begin to believe they were created and saved to multiply the church and change the world.

Our drummer at church recently shared about leading the lead singer of a world-famous rock band to Jesus just three days before he died. Drumming is a great help to church worship, but **IT BECOMES PRIESTLY WORK WHEN IT IS USED TO HELP SPREAD THE SEED OF THE GOSPEL.**

I've been convicted time and time again when I watched people who were sitting on the sidelines at our church go with one of our church-planting teams and turn into dynamic, priestly leaders. We had them handing out bulletins, and now they're laying hands on the sick and seeing miracles. They are teaching, discipling, evangelizing, interceding. Multiplication placed the demand and the expectation on them, and they rose up to their priestly calling.

Too often, ordinary lay people disqualify themselves because they have only seen church done in one particular way and they think they could never do "that." Our church models set up high standards which are unrealistic for the normal believer. We need an assortment of models.

CONSIDER THIS: WHAT TYPE OF EQUIPPING IS MOST COMMON IN YOUR CHURCH?

Eighteenth century Methodism was a lay movement. Although there were always clergy exercising some overall guidance—John and Charles Wesley, and John Fletcher most notably—the movement depended on laity who would take the lead and make decisions in a wide variety of contexts.

---

17   Dr. Art Lindsley, "*The Priesthood of All Believers*," Institute for Faith, Work and Economics, October 15, 2013, https://tifwe.org/resource/the-priesthood-of-all-believers (accessed June 17, 2016).

There were, first of all, the itinerating lay preachers, assigned in pairs to circuits throughout the British Isles, and eventually sent in pairs to America. There were also the non-itinerating local ministers and the stewards who oversaw the various societies. Most important were the leaders of classes, who provided spiritual oversight for those under their care.

What Wesley did was open the door for hundreds of men and women to become leaders in the vast missionary endeavor of spreading scriptural holiness across the nation. Since most of these leaders were not from the upper classes, British society did not provide avenues of leadership. Indeed, some evangelical pastors criticized Wesley for disrespecting the class distinctions they wrongly believed God had established. But Wesley recognized their gifts and commitment, and enlisted them into God's service.[18]

If newer believers of average intelligence with no formal theological education can't be unleashed as star players on your team, then your game plan is misguided. If you have to wait for people of unusual talent or extensive schooling or extraordinary spiritual gifting, then you are signing up for a slow addition model of ministry.

Often leaders with these attributes may create a splash in one location but actually slow the overall work down. As Alan Briggs, the director of Frontline Church Planting, says, **"JESUS NEVER SENT OUT THE SCRIBES AND PHARISEES. THEY KNEW TOO MUCH AND OBEYED TOO LITTLE."**[19]

Too many pastors want to limit and employ church members instead of launch and deploy them into the harvest. The pastor is building his/her local church vision and needs workers to help construct it, so the goal of release is threatening.

MOST CHURCHES ARE BEING BUILT BY PROFESSIONAL CONTRACTORS USING AN ADDITION MODEL.
In most addition models the slogan is: WE CAN BUILD IT, YOU CAN HELP.

I believe God wants his church to be built by non-professionals using a multiplication model. Home Depot's slogan from 2003 to 2009 is a good one for the church. In multiplication models the slogan is: YOU CAN BUILD IT, WE CAN HELP!

This model happens when the birds are set free to fly. The church is a branch for the bird to rest upon and even to call home; the mission, however, goes beyond the branch. **THE MISSION IS THE SEED BEING SOWN IN THE WORLD.**

---

18   Henry H. Knight III, "*Wesley and Lay Leadership: Church Renewal, Wesley and the Methodists,*" Catalyst Resources, February 1, 2011, http://www.catalystresources.org/consider-wesley-51/ (accessed June 17, 2016)
19   Alan Briggs, as quoted on Missional Communities, October 26, 2015, https://www.facebook.com/permalink.php?id=197077533657897&story_fbid=1020499251315717 (accessed June 17, 2016).

This unleashing must include the equipping Ephesians 4:11-12 emphasizes. **SKILLS, TOOLS AND PROVISIONS WILL EMPOWER THE ORDINARY PERSON TO SERVE IN AN EFFECTIVE KINGDOM ROLE.** Pastors must provide this kind of equipping so saints can "do the work of ministry," and believing, ordinary saints can change the world.

CONSIDER THIS: DO YOU SEE YOURSELF AS PART OF THE PRIESTHOOD? IN WHAT WAYS CAN YOU DO MORE FRONTLINE SPIRITUAL MINISTRY?

Deb and I escaped Hurricane Patricia. We had joined our friends in Puerto Vallarta for five days of resting and writing at the Grand Mayan Resort. Three days into our time there, we learned that the most powerful hurricane ever measured was headed right for us. We had a choice to make: Drive our rental car inland eight hours to Guadalajara or stay to try to help in what would surely be a tragic natural disaster? Our hearts told us to stay. But when we saw how we were equipped, we thought differently. We had flip-flops and beachwear. **WE WERE PREPARED FOR RESORT LIVING INSTEAD OF A RESCUE MISSION.** With that reality check, we escaped to relative safety.

Often Christians are told to go on a rescue mission, but pastors have only provided flip-flops and beachwear. Disciples are being trained for their Christian resorts (churches) but not for the rescue mission in their neighborhood.

When saints begin to envision themselves as priests, I'm confident their multiplication imagination will be ignited. As they are properly equipped to fly they will begin to unleash their movement-making potential.

QUESTIONS TO CONSIDER:

1. What level of skills and training would a person need to lead in your current model of church?

2. Have you seen God use an unlikely person in unexpected ways?

3. What kind of positions are most volunteers recruited for?

4. What type of equipping is most common in your church?

5. Do you see yourself as part of the priesthood? In what ways can you do more frontline spiritual ministry?

CHAPTER EIGHT: VARIETY

WE BELIEVE IN
EMPOWERING ALL THE
GIFTS OF THE SPIRIT
AND DEPLOYING ALL THE
DIVERSITY IN THE CHURCH
TO FUEL MULTIPLICATION.

I CORINTHIANS 12:4-6 "There are different kinds of gifts, but the same Spirit distributes them. There are different kinds of service, but the same Lord. There are different kinds of working, but in all of them and in everyone it is the same God at work."

God loves and uses diversity. Mustard plants exist in many varieties which thrive in different locations and are used for various purposes. Primarily there are white/yellow, brown, and black mustard seeds. They are each "precious in his sight." Each of these have particular strengths and uses.

Yellow/White mustard seeds: These are the most mellow. You can find them in your everything bagel for texture.

Brown mustard seeds: These are used for a stronger bite and are often found mixed with yellow seeds in a wholegrain style mustard.

Black mustard seeds: These are the strongest. If you simply add water and let the mixture sit overnight, you'll have some super-hot mustard on your hands.

Jesus may not have had diversity in mind when he used mustard as a metaphor for the kingdom, but it certainly fits. The Mustard Seed Tribe prioritizes variety. **MULTIPLICATION DEMANDS THE FULL EMPLOYMENT OF ALL THE GIFTS AVAILABLE TO THE CHURCH.**

CONSIDER THIS: HOW DIVERSE IN AGE, ETHNICITY AND PERSONALITY IS YOUR CIRCLE OF FRIENDS?

One of our church members, Beau Crosetto, has written a widely distributed book on personal evangelism. Beau is a leader with the campus ministry InterVarsity, working with all the campuses in Southern California. Beau has shared his faith thousands of times with all types of people. It is from these experiences that Beau has titled his book, Beyond Awkward.

My friend, Ben, on the other hand, is brilliant with a gift of teaching. He can understand complex issues and explain them in understandable ways. Unlike Beau, Ben is a major introvert who finds it difficult to talk with people about anything, especially significant personal matters like faith. Every conversation for Ben is awkward, but often Ben will bust through his discomfort and share Jesus with people.

Beau would be proud of Ben. Beau shares that just because it's awkward doesn't mean we stop; instead **WE LISTEN TO HOW THE LORD WOULD WANT US TO LOVE AND COMMUNICATE WITH THE PERSON IN FRONT OF US.** There are a variety of approaches, but they all stem from the same place – authentic love for the individual.

Beau has a gift of evangelism, but he's also just obedient. Ben has the gift of teaching, but he evangelizes because he also is committed to obey. **EVANGELISM ISN'T ONLY THE RESPONSIBILITY OF THE GIFTED; IT IS THE DUTY OF EVERY BELIEVER.** (If you missed it, I just called you by name...and me, too.)

Ben would miss his call if he didn't major in his teaching gift, but he would disobey his duty if he didn't seek to share Jesus when he found opportunities to do so.

While Beau promotes evangelism, he is a big believer in the four other ministry giftings listed in Ephesians 4:11. In fact, he has a blog entitled Release the APE. Let me explain the creative title.

It is derived from Ephesians 4:11: "So Christ himself gave the apostles, the prophets, the evangelists, the pastors and teachers." The church in America has been Shepherd (pastor)/Teacher centric. The weakness of that reality is it marginalizes the other three gifts of Ephesians 4:11. To the church in America, evangelists are people like Billy Graham or Greg Laurie. Apostles are extinct or rarer than swimsuits in Alaska. Prophets are weird and bothersome.

A Shepherd/Teacher model somewhat works in a culturally Christian nation. Why? Because the primary job is simply caring for and instructing those who probably believe in God and the Bible anyway.

The challenge comes in a post-Christian nation (i.e. our current culture). Without the other three giftings being actively employed, the numbers of new converts and new churches begin to shrink. There are few apostles to start new networks of churches; minimal evangelists persuading people to place their faith in Christ and equipping other believers to evangelize; scarce prophets to reveal, convince, and goad toward truth, justice, and mercy.

Beau's passion is to see us "Release the APE" – the Apostle, Prophet, Evangelist. His conviction is that we need this to happen to see a gospel and church planting movement in America. **UNLESS WE EMBRACE THE DIVERSITY OF THE GIFTS AND OF THE PEOPLE WHO EXPRESS THEM, WE WILL BE STUCK IN OUR CURRENT REALITY OF LOSING KINGDOM TERRITORY IN AMERICA.**

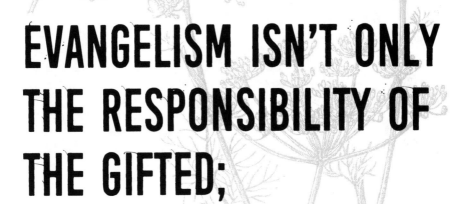

EVANGELISM ISN'T ONLY THE RESPONSIBILITY OF THE GIFTED;

IT IS THE DUTY OF EVERY BELIEVER

Alan Hirsch does an excellent job of summarizing these Ephesians 4:11 gifts in his book The Forgotten Ways:

APOSTLES extend the gospel. As the sent ones, they ensure that the faith is transmitted from one context to another and from one generation to the next. They are always thinking about the future, bridging barriers, establishing the church in new contexts, developing leaders, networking trans-locally. Yes, if you focus solely on initiating new ideas and rapid expansion, you can leave people and organizations wounded. The shepherding and teaching functions are needed to ensure people are cared for rather than simply used.

PROPHETS know God's will. They are particularly attuned to God and his truth for today. They bring correction and challenge the dominant assumptions we inherit from the culture. They insist that the community obey what God has commanded. They question the status quo. Without the other types of leaders in place, prophets can become belligerent activists or, paradoxically, disengage from the imperfection of reality and become other-worldly.

EVANGELISTS recruit. These infectious communicators of the gospel message recruit others to the cause. They call for a personal response to God's redemption in Christ, and also draw believers to engage the wider mission, growing the church. Evangelists can be so focused on reaching those outside the church that maturing and strengthening those inside is neglected.

SHEPHERDS nurture and protect. Caregivers of the community, they focus on the protection and spiritual maturity of God's flock, cultivating a loving and spiritually mature network of relationships, making and developing disciples. Shepherds can value stability to the detriment of the mission. They may also foster an unhealthy dependence between the church and themselves.

TEACHERS understand and explain. Communicators of God's truth and wisdom, they help others remain biblically grounded to better discern God's will, guiding others toward wisdom, helping the community remain faithful to Christ's word, and constructing a transferable doctrine. Without the input of the other functions, teachers can fall into dogmatism or dry intellectualism. They may fail to see the personal or missional aspects of the church's ministry.[20]

---

20 "What is APEST?", The Forgotten Ways, http://www.theforgottenways.org/what-is-apest.aspx (accessed June 20, 2016).

DO YOU KNOW YOUR GIFTS? Followers of Jesus tend to be wired and gifted for one or two of these five giftings. While all believers have the Spirit of Christ indwelling them and may express any of the gifts, they will generally default towards one or two of these strengths.

CONSIDER THIS: OF THE FIVE MAJOR GIFTS OF EPHESIANS 4:11, WHICH OF THEM WOULD BEST DESCRIBE YOU? WHICH WOULD LEAST DESCRIBE YOU?

The discovery and deployment of spiritual gifts is a vital component of seeing multiplication through your life, your ministry, or your church. **DISCIPLES MUST BE READY TO DO THEIR DUTY IN ALL SITUATIONS**, to hear and obey the voice of the Lord, to receive and minister the gift needed in the moment. At the same time, they must major in the area of giftedness God has endowed them with. Being trapped in areas of ministry which don't fit your giftings leads to frustration instead of fruitfulness.

Apostles are especially gifted at catalyzing movements. Multiplication thinking comes naturally to them. They are always starting something fresh and recruiting new leaders into the movement. They are fired up to launch the next ministry, group, church. **WE MUST GIVE SPECIAL ATTENTION TO EMPOWERING THE GIFT OF APOSTLE IN OUR CHURCHES** if we want to see multiplication occur.

The variety is not only in the full engagement of all the gifts of the church, it is in the diversity of the messengers who deliver the gifts. To be a movement we need ministers who represent wealth/poverty, male/female, black/brown/white, 20-something/70-something, natives/immigrants/undocumented, educated/illiterate. Each of these identity descriptions become subordinate to anointing, calling, gifting, truth-telling, compassion, passion and surrender. **MULTIPLICATION IS NOT MAJORING IN THE DUPLICATION OF PEOPLE WHO LOOK, SOUND, AND THINK LIKE YOU.**

Twenty-five years ago our church, Light & Life, was only one type of "mustard" – white. We were a handful of Anglos who were living in a multiethnic neighborhood. Diversify or die was our reality. We were clueless about how to build a multiethnic church, but we knew how to pray. We started praying a specific prayer, "Lord, help our church look like our neighborhood." Simultaneously, we began to ask God what steps to take to build this kind of church.

God answered our prayers in dramatic ways. In 2011 Leadership Network recognized our church as one of the most diverse churches in America. It wasn't a pain-free journey by any means. Along the way we lost some of our wealthy white members who were no longer comfortable in this kind of church.

But we gained so many amazing individuals who expressed their gifts in unique ways to spread the gospel: rappers with rhymes, dancers with hip-hop, Mexicans with mariachi, Africans with headdresses, Polynesians with hula dances, Cambodians with survival stories, Indonesians with delicious nasi goreng, African Americans with gospel, and Anglos with jazz. All of these and many others came together and are being used by God.

Many who visit our church from more segregated or less diverse areas tell us after service, "This is what heaven will look like." Although we are a long way from fitting that description, I do know our diversity has served our multiplication vision.

CONSIDER THIS: HOW ETHNICALLY DIVERSE IS THE TWENTY-MINUTE DRIVING CIRCUMFERENCE OF YOUR CHURCH? HOW ABOUT THE TEN-MINUTE WALKING CIRCUMFERENCE? HOW CLOSE IS YOUR CHURCH TO REFLECTING THAT DIVERSITY IN THE CONGREGATION AND ESPECIALLY IN THE LEADERSHIP?

Psalm 133 describes how good and enjoyable it is when diverse brothers and sisters come together, live together, worship together, and serve together in unity. God tells us this kind of unity will attract his anointing and his blessing.

If we are serious about multiplication in America **WE MUST ALSO BECOME URGENT ABOUT THE FULL EMPOWERMENT OF WOMEN INTO MINISTRY.** Imagine going into a boxing match against the late Muhammed Ali and being told you can only throw punches with your right hand. Ali could "float like a butterfly, sting like a bee" but you could only strike with your right; your left punch needed to be left behind. You would be set up for defeat.

A similar scenario is being lived out in the church of Jesus. Women have been marginalized and minimized on this mission. Men will fight the battle and women can hang around to support. The left hand is as strong as the right, but male referees have been reluctant to fully release it into the fight.

Yet, at the start of the church, God seems to anticipate this inequity by emphasizing the egalitarian nature of his mission force. Acts 2, the chapter detailing the church's opening day, has plenty to say about empowering women. Acts 2:17-18 declares, "'In the last days,' God says, 'I will pour out my Spirit on all people. Your sons and daughters will prophesy, your young men will see visions, your old men will dream dreams. Even on my servants, both men and women, I will pour out my Spirit in those days, and they will prophesy.'"

There are multiple ways women may be constrained. Even if a group's theology embraces the full-empowerment of women, existing power structures may be daunting hurdles. Predefined roles assigned by society and not by God can limit women. The lack of benevolent male advocates who not only believe in egalitarianism, but who seek practical ways to support it, can hold women back. Men who struggle to control their own lust can wrongly view women as temptresses and restrict them due to their own fear.

CONSIDER THIS: HOW DOES YOUR CHURCH LEADERSHIP REFLECT THE GIFTEDNESS AND EQUALITY OF WOMEN?

We must press through any practice or structure which restricts the full giftedness of women. **BT ROBERTS, OUR FREE METHODIST FOUNDER, SAW THE ORDINATION AND FULL DEPLOYMENT OF WOMEN AS A KEY DOCTRINE FOR THE SPREAD OF THE GOSPEL.** This fight for truth cannot be won with half of the army sequestered to the barracks or mess hall.

Light & Life has started a network of churches among the remote islands of the Bicol region of the Philippines. While we have many fruitful pastors there, our most apostolic pastor is Pastora Isabela. Not only has she grown one of our largest churches, she has started several others. Hundreds are coming to faith as a result of her ministry. She has multiplied herself several time already. She has taken the gospel and begun churches in areas no male pastor had previously reached.

Prioritizing the diversity of gifts, of ethnicities and of genders creates an atmosphere where multiplication can thrive.

CONSIDER THIS: WHAT ACTION STEPS CAN YOU OR YOUR CHURCH TAKE TO MORE GREATLY DIVERSIFY YOUR LIFE AND MINISTRY?

QUESTIONS TO CONSIDER:

1. How diverse in age, ethnicity, and personality is your circle of friends?

2. Of the five major gifts of Ephesians 4:11, which of them would best describe you? Which would least describe you?

3. How ethnically diverse is the twenty-minute driving circumference of your church? How about the ten-minute walking circumference? How close is your church to reflecting that diversity in the congregation and especially in the leadership?

4. How does your church leadership reflect the giftedness and equality of women?

5. What action steps can you or your church take to more greatly diversify your life and ministry?

CHAPTER NINE: SEED PODS

Tab. IV.

WE BELIEVE DISCIPLES GATHER IN ORDER TO GROW AND GO.

ACTS 13:3 "So after they had fasted and prayed, they placed their hands on them and sent them off."

Mustard plants do not multiply by generating seeds, at least not initially. They multiply by first producing seed pods. In these pods seeds grow and develop. As the seed pods mature the seeds inside of them do, also. Some seedpods have a few seeds, others have dozens. Eventually, the seed pods burst open, releasing their seeds to reproduce and multiply, spreading their beauty broadly.

The purpose of the seed pod is to cover the seeds as they are growing, so that in a short time they can be sent to the earth. The seed pod's effectiveness is not based on how many seeds are in the pod, but by whether these seeds are sent to multiply.

I love the local church. I love the global church. I believe that Christ through the local church is the hope of my city and our world. **THE POWER INHERENT WHEN DISCIPLES GATHER TO WORSHIP, LEARN, AND PRAY IS SUPERNATURAL.** Jesus himself promised His manifested presence when believers gather in the authority of and for the glory of His name (Matthew 18:20). Or like a preacher once quipped, "If two or three believers can ever agree on anything, Jesus himself will show up to see it."

CONSIDER THIS: DO YOU SENSE THE PRESENCE OF GOD IN YOUR MIDST WHEN YOUR CHURCH GATHERS FOR WORSHIP?

The power is there in the gathering for a season and for a reason. If the same saints get together week after week, year after year, only to worship, learn, and pray, then the power stops flowing. The power season is over because the gathering missed its reason for existence. If the disciples don't go do what they are learning, then they stop maturing and start spoiling. These are the "dead branches" Jesus speaks of in John 15:2, which he lops off due to their fruitlessness.

Seed pods spoil when they cling to their seeds in possessiveness or fear. Churches forfeit the presence and power of Jesus when the gathering, instead of the mission, becomes the focus of the church.

CONSIDER THIS: DOES IT SEEM THAT YOUR CHURCH PRIORITIZES GATHERING MORE THAN EQUIPPING PEOPLE TO GO?

WE ARE NOT SAVED TO SIT;

WE ARE SAVED TO BE SENT

As evangelist Charles Spurgeon bluntly pointed out 150 years ago, "Every Christian is either a missionary or an impostor." For our time we might clarify that language to say, "Every Christian must live out the mission of God or be recognized as a hypocrite." **WE ARE NOT SAVED TO SIT; WE ARE SAVED TO BE SENT.**

Thirty-three times in the gospel of John, Jesus uses two short words to describe who he is and what he is doing in the world. Those two words, "sent me," encapsulate Jesus' self-understanding. **HE IS A MAN ON A MISSION FOR GOD.** Period. Near the very end of John's gospel, Jesus passes that same mantel on to us individually and collectively when he says, "As the Father has sent me, I am sending you" (John 20:21).

To be the church of Jesus we must fully embrace this identity. We are "sent ones." To be missional the church realizes its essence is to join Jesus on his mission to save and heal a broken world.

CONSIDER THIS: ACCORDING TO JOHN'S GOSPEL WE ARE TO LIVE AS "SENT ONES." HOW ARE YOU LIVING OUT THIS CALL? TO WHOM DO YOU BELIEVE GOD HAS SENT YOU?

As Ed Stetzer writes, "Mission is rooted in the identity of God Himself. God is on a mission, and Jesus is the embodiment of that mission...**THE CHURCH IS SENT ON MISSION BY JESUS.** It's not that the church has a mission, but rather that the mission has a church."[21]

I grew from birth to adulthood in rural Kansas. Twenty-five miles from my hometown is a church next to a feedlot. This feedlot houses 100,000 head of cattle who stand at their feed trough, eating and taking care of biological business just across the road. The wonderful church folks there say the odor filling the air smells like money. I had quite a different way of describing it. These cattle are enjoying the good life, the safe life inside their own pen with daily deliveries of food...until the butcher shows up.

---

21   Ed Stetzer, *"God's Mission has a Church: My Interview with Tabletalk Magazine,"* Christianity Today, January 29, 2014, http://www.christianitytoday.com/edstetzer/2014/january/my-interview-with-tabletalk-magazine.html (Accessed June 20, 2016).

I've known this church for over five decades, and I have noticed something. It is not the result of research but of casual observation. **WHENEVER THIS CHURCH IS OUTWARDLY FOCUSED AND SENDING MONEY AND PEOPLE ON MISSION, IT THRIVES.** Not even the off-putting aroma can hold the church back. But when it becomes fixated on its own struggles, squabbles and pleasures, it begins to shrivel. It has its own repugnant smell.

Of course their condition is not an either/or situation. Their vitality is on a continuum that seems linked to their faith and external focus. I believe this is true whether we are speaking of the health of a disciple, a small group, or a church. External focus exudes the aroma of Christ.

One of the tallest hurdles for the church is the fallacy that you must grow before you go, instead of understanding you will grow as you go. Jesus very quickly gave his disciples missional assignments and then debriefed them based on how it went (e.g. Luke 10). **IT IS THE MISSION WHICH CREATES THE OPPORTUNITIES FOR MATURING.**

Instead, too often the American idea of church has been to line up the saints at the spiritual feed trough every Sunday. The goal is to over feed them, under exercise them, and keep them safely corralled until Jesus comes.

CONSIDER THIS: IS THE ATMOSPHERE OF YOUR CHURCH MARKED MORE BY INSECURITY OR GENEROSITY?

The Antioch church wasn't near a feedlot, but it was just five miles from the pleasure resort of Daphne. Daphne, a suburb of Antioch, might be compared to modern day Las Vegas. If there was a place that the church might choose to circle the wagons, isolate, and hold off the enemy until Jesus came, it was in Antioch.

But this was not the story the church at Antioch would write. Instead, it was here that the disciples were first called Christians, perhaps indicating their bold witness in the city. It was Antioch that would become the first center of Gentile Christianity.

Undoubtedly, one of the reasons for such influence was the missional priority the Antioch church lived on. The Antioch church was not going to sit around the proverbial campfire singing "Kum Ba Yah." They were on mission with Jesus. They gathered together to fast and pray about the mission. They gathered in order to go. The analogy of church gatherings to football huddles has rightly been applied often.

The huddle in American football is a vital part of the game. It is where the next play is called, players are positioned, information about the enemy is exchanged, and encouragement is given. Huddles are essential, and if you miss them you will end up on the bench and eventually off the team. But the game of football is neither played nor won in the huddle, but at the scrimmage line. The huddle exists for the purpose of the mission. Discipleship, small groups, and churches who forget this soon find themselves losing instead of winning, spoiling instead of maturing.

Acts 13:1-3 describes the "huddle" at Antioch: "Now in the church at Antioch there were prophets and teachers: Barnabas, Simeon called Niger, Lucius of Cyrene, Manaen (who had been brought up with Herod the tetrarch) and Saul. While they were worshiping the Lord and fasting, the Holy Spirit said, 'SET APART FOR ME BARNABAS AND SAUL FOR THE WORK TO WHICH I HAVE CALLED THEM.' So after they had fasted and prayed, they placed their hands on them and sent them off."

Note that the church's worship and fasting didn't just lead to goosebumps or holier living. It positioned them to hear the call for the next play. Now the star players on the Antioch team were Barnabas and Saul; nevertheless, the Antioch church blessed them and sent them to another town to start a new team. Antioch could have stayed with addition, but instead it multiplied. Antioch was a church on mission.

Multiplication stems from Christians, groups, and churches who believe in the power of gathering but also in the priority of sending; it's a both/and. The gathering is organized around the mission. **THE MISSION IS NOT AN APPENDAGE TO THE GATHERING BUT THE HEART OF THE GATHERING.**

Some have misunderstood me as being a church growth opponent. Nothing is further from the truth. As a pastor, I am trying to lead my church to growth every week. As a superintendent, I love missional communities of a dozen people, and I celebrate megachurches with their thousands. I am friends with pastors of both. I am very opposed, however, to churches organized around addition instead of mission. If the primary effort is put into answering the question "How can we gather more people?" instead of "How can we send more people?" then the church has missed the priority of Jesus.

CONSIDER THIS: CONSIDER YOUR CHURCH'S MISSION STATEMENT. DOES IT REFLECT RELEASING, GIVING AWAY, OR SENDING? HOW COULD IT CHANGE TO BETTER REFLECT THESE PRIORITIES?

How can you tell whether your group or church is prioritizing sending over gathering? Use these 15 questions as a guide.

I. IS THE KEY LEADERSHIP SOLD OUT TO THE PRIORITY OF SENDING?
As the leader goes, so goes the church.

2. IS THE CONCEPT OF SENDING BEING PUT INTO UNDERSTANDABLE AND COMPELLING LANGUAGE?
One of the best ways to find this out is to see if you can give an "Elevator Speech" (60 seconds) about what your church is seeking to accomplish.

3. IS THE MISSION AND SENDING PEOPLE OUT A CONSISTENT PRIORITY IN TIMES OF PRAYER?
For our church, every new act of sending has been preceded by an intense time of prayer and often fasting.

4. IS THE MISSION AND SENDING PEOPLE OUT A FREQUENT TEACHING IN THE PULPIT OR GROUP?
Do a quick review of the last 30 sermons. How much is there about getting the church outside the building to serve? How much is there about the call to start something new?

5. IS A PLAN IN PLACE OR BEING WORKED ON FOR HOW TO MULTIPLY YOUR GROUP OR CHURCH?
My first lead pastor in ministry had this sign above his desk – "Fail to plan, plan to fail."

6. ARE INSPIRING STORIES ABOUT SENDING BEING TOLD PUBLICALLY AND/OR RELATIONALLY?
People are changed by the stories you tell. When you tell stories of people in your church living out the mission or tell of other churches sending out people, it influences people.

7. HAS THE MISSION STATEMENT OF THE CHURCH BEEN ENGINEERED AROUND SENDING?
When we changed our mission statement to – "Reach, Teach, Mend, Send" – it gave our people a saying they could hold onto about what we were doing. It's a continual rallying cry for us.

8. IS THIS SENDING VALUE CLEARLY TAUGHT IN YOUR MEMBERSHIP CLASS?
Our priority on being a sending church was right up front and very clear in our membership class. We wanted people to know they were signing up for a very rare kind of church.

9. ARE POTENTIAL NEW GROUP LEADERS OR NEW CHURCH PLANTERS GIVEN PUBLIC OPPORTUNITIES?

If a church rarely sees anyone in the pulpit or leading the group except the senior pastor or group leader, it will be difficult to believe people are being raised up to be sent out.

10. WHAT IS THE SCOREBOARD OF THE CHURCH SET UP TO RECORD AND CELEBRATE?

Who are the biggest heroes in your church? Are they the people who are volunteering inside the church or the people extending God's mission outside the church?

11. WHAT GETS TOP BILLING IN THE CHURCH BUDGET?

We started budgeting for a church plant two years before we could get our first church plant sent out the door. We wanted our people to know we were willing to sacrifice for the mission even before it was a reality.

12. IS THE VISION CLEARLY UNDERSTOOD AND SUPPORTED BY THE AVERAGE CHURCH ATTENDEE?

Vision is different from mission in that people can see it and describe the key characteristics of the future in their own words. Most of our people can describe what a "River" church is that is sending people out.

13. IS THE DISTINCTION BETWEEN DONATING MONEY AND DOING MINISTRY BEING CLEARLY ARTICULATED WITH A PRIORITY UPON THE DOING?

Many churches think they are missional because of their generous financial support for ministry. While such a reality is highly commendable, it is not a church of multiplication and may actually serve as an excuse for people to not do the work of ministry.

14. IS THERE A FEELING OF HIGH CONTROL OR HIGH FREEDOM IN THE CHURCH?

If leaders are insecure and fearful, they will be reluctant to encourage people to freely listen for God's guidance about their mission. We teach people to listen for God's mission and know we will cheer them on.

15. HOW LONG WOULD IT TAKE THE CITY LEADERS TO NOTICE IF THE CHURCH STOPPED OPERATING?

If the church is stuck inside its building and members are mainly serving the needs of the church, then not much is missing from the community if the church moves or closes. Our best awards have not come from Christians, but from the city.

GOD WANTS OUR MUSTARD SEED PODS NOT TO ROT ON THE BRANCH BUT RELEASE THEIR SEEDS to multiply gospel proclaiming ministries and churches.

QUESTIONS TO CONSIDER:

1. Do you sense the presence of God in your midst when your church gathers for worship?

2. Does it seem that your church prioritizes gathering more than equipping people to go?

3. According to John's gospel we are to live as "sent ones." How are you living out this call? To whom do you believe God has sent you?

4. Is the atmosphere of your church marked more by insecurity or generosity?

5. Consider your church's mission statement. Does it reflect releasing, giving away, or sending? How could it change to better reflect these priorities?

CHAPTER TEN: NEMATODES

WE BELIEVE MULTIPLICATION IS ADVANCED THROUGH STRATEGIC PRAYER.

EPHESIANS 6:19 "Pray also for me, that whenever I speak, words may be given me so that I will fearlessly make known the mystery of the gospel."

I could make a good horror movie out of nematodes. Imagine this: a snake-like being with a vicious mouth. Inside that mouth is a sharp needle-like structure called a stylet. The stylet acts like a hypodermic needle to pierce through the skull and suck the brain out of its victim.

Before you close this book and run, let me give you the rest of the story. What I have just described is a plant-feeding nematode. It is less than one millimeter long and nearly invisible to the naked eye. It lives in the soil and attacks the cells of living plants like grapevines or pine trees. But don't underestimate them, as they are deadly. For example, the pine wilt nematode has caused the death of tens of millions of pine trees in Japan.

There is one thing that causes the nematodes to flee - spicy mustard plants. This is why many gardeners, vintners, and arborists plant mustard in between their rows. They even breed special strains of mustard to increase their spiciness and make them more effective.

NEMATODES ARE AN EXCELLENT METAPHOR FOR DEMONS. Demons come to steal, kill, and destroy (John 10:10). They like to work beneath the surface, silently attacking anything that will bear fruit for Jesus. They seek to steal the truth from the minds of Christians in an effort to diminish their effectiveness. They hate the potential of multiplication and will undermine it and distract from it in any way possible.

The Mustard Seed Tribe, however, claims the power of Luke 10:19: "I have given you authority to trample on snakes and scorpions and to overcome all the power of the enemy; nothing will harm you." You could insert "nematodes" in this verse. **DISCIPLES LIVING IN THE GENUINE AUTHORITY OF JESUS HAVE A POWER TO "RESIST THE DEVIL** and he will flee from you" (James 4:7).

This authority is exercised through strategic prayer. As I observe the church, prayer is more assumed than activated, more presumed than practiced, more taught than wrought, more of a theology than an implemented strategy. **THE ENEMY IS SILENTLY UNDERMINING OUR EFFECTIVENESS** and we respond by trying harder or instituting new programs.

CONSIDER THIS: WHAT HAS BEEN YOUR EXPERIENCE IN ENGAGING THE SPIRITUAL REALM OF DARKNESS?

When God called our church, Light and Life, to start planting new churches, we were basically clueless as to how to do it. The city of Long Beach, with its half a million residents, is such a diverse and unchurched city we had no idea where to plant the first church or who should plant it. What we did know how to do was pray.

Consequently, we started by calling a 40-Day Fast. Most of the church participated and fasted something significant. Out of that time it was revealed that I should plant the first church. That path seemed logical and foolish. It was logical in that if we were going to major in church planting it would help if I had actually planted a church (this is not a necessity but is helpful). It was foolish in that I was already preaching three services on Sunday and quite busy.

My wife Deb, daughter Lindsey, and I lived in a far different part of the city than where our existing church was. Not only was our home twenty minutes from the church, it was radically different demographically – white, proud, upper-class people with a reliance upon their advanced university degrees. It was also grossly under-churched. Thankfully, our gifted youth pastors, JR and Kim Rushik, felt led to assist us in this first planting adventure.

We gathered three others and we started to pray. We knew the enemy had specific strongholds over this neighborhood, and we began to counterattack through prayer. Deb and I had been prayer walking the main street of the area for several years, asking God to bring salvation. Now we added others to these prayer walks. JR and I bicycled around the perimeters of this area of town doing prayer rides. We recruited a core team of 25 and our primary priority was prayer. We had all night prayer meetings on more than one occasion.

The result? When we had our opening night service, over fifty new people from the neighborhood showed up to check us out. Twenty of them ended up staying, and a new church was launched there that grew to over 150 in attendance. Perhaps even more importantly, the church ended up launching several other pastors and ministry leaders. One of those leaders became one of the most influential Christians among the Congressional leaders in Washington, D.C.

WHAT IS YOUR PRAYER STRATEGY?

CONSIDER THIS: HOW WOULD YOU DESCRIBE YOUR PRAYER LIFE ON BEHALF OF THE MISSION OF GOD?

When coaching church planters one of my first questions is: **WHAT IS YOUR PRAYER STRATEGY?** If they don't have a plan for a concerted prayer effort, it signals me as to whose efforts they are depending on. They have falsely assumed they can overcome the destructive "nematodes" on their own power.

Ephesians 6 should be the starting chapter for anyone who wants to multiply disciples, groups, ministries, or churches. Paul spends the first five chapters of Ephesians giving us soaring theology of the mystery of Christ, then deeply rooting those truths in our practical daily living. As he concludes his letter, he points to the spiritual attack that will seek to divide the truth of Ephesians 1-3 from the lifestyle and ministry of Ephesians 3-6.

Paul unveils the spiritual powers opposing our efforts to turn our beliefs into behaviors which bless our lives and build God's kingdom. He reminds us **THERE IS AN UNSEEN ADVERSARY WHO HATES OUR MINISTRY AND WILL SEEK TO UNDERMINE IT.**

This is such a priority and passion for Paul that **HE PLEADS WITH THEM TO PRAY FOR HIM PERSONALLY** – "Pray also for me, that whenever I speak, words may be given me so that I will fearlessly make known the mystery of the gospel" (Ephesians 6:19). Paul is saying, "I know my mission and my intention BUT there is an evil force seeking to limit me and bind me in fear. Therefore, please join me in prayer that I may overcome."

It is this demonic resistance that must be resisted, not as an afterthought but as a forethought. **PAUL WAS SEEKING PARTNERS WHO WOULD SEND THEIR PRAYERS AHEAD OF HIM** so when the opportunities for sharing the gospel occurred, the enemy could not hold him back through fear.

Too many Christians don't pray against the enemy until they feel an attack. Even then their first inclination is to reason it away by assigning blame to anything other than the evil one. As a last resort they decide to pray against the devil.

However, when Jesus taught us to pray in Matthew 6:9-13, he taught a daily prayer (e.g. "give us this day our daily bread") that included a petition for daily deliverance from "the evil one." The implication is **THERE WILL BE A DAILY ATTACK BY OUR SPIRITUAL ENEMY AND RESISTANCE THROUGH DAILY PRAYER IS VITAL.**

Personally, I call this type of prayer "making space for ministry." By starting the day with a direct request against the devil, I believe I send a blocker ahead to make space for me to carry the gospel through. In football, if I have the ball, there is someone out to resist me, tackle me, and thwart my goal of advancement. But prayer can block the enemy for me and open a "hole" for me to run through. It can create space for ministry to happen and allow for missional advancement.

CONSIDER THIS: IN WHAT WAYS DO YOU EXERCISE DIRECT AUTHORITY AGAINST THE FORCES OF EVIL?

WE MUST NEITHER OVERESTIMATE NOR MARGINALIZE DEMONIC INFLUENCE AGAINST OUR MULTIPLICATION EFFORTS. C.S. Lewis is helpful when he writes, in The Screwtape Letters, "There are two equal and opposite errors into which our race can fall about the devils. One is to disbelieve in their existence. The other is to believe, and to feel an excessive and unhealthy interest in them. They themselves are equally pleased by both errors and hail a materialist or a magician with the same delight."[22]

Prayer which takes authority against the evil one to make space for ministry is called spiritual warfare prayer. This kind of prayer is essential in multiplying ministry because when you pursue this vision it marks you for special attention from the devil. You become a high value target to Satan.

Gary Larson, one of the great American cartoonists of the 20th Century, drew a cartoon of two deer in the forest standing on their back legs. One of the deer has a large red target with a bullseye on his chest. The other deer says, "Bummer of a birthmark, Hal." I often think of this when we begin to plant another church. It feels like we've just drawn the target on our chest.

PRAYER PARTNERSHIPS, ESPECIALLY TRIADS (THREE PEOPLE UNIFYING IN PRAYER), ARE HIGHLY EFFECTIVE IN RESISTING THE ENEMY SO MINISTRY CAN HAPPEN. These prayer partnerships take their cue from Ecclesiastes 4:12: "Though one may be overpowered, two can defend themselves. A cord of three strands is not quickly broken."

---

22   C.S. Lewis, as quoted in Mere C.S. Lewis, July 26, 2010, http://merecslewis.blogspot.com/2010/07/two-mistaken-views-christians-have.html, (accessed June 24, 2016).

The power of unified prayer is symbolized in Exodus 17. In this passage, the Israelites are winning their battle with the Amalekites as long as Moses has his anointed shepherd's rod lifted into the air. However, when the staff comes down, the Israelites start to go down in defeat. This is when Aaron and Hur partnered with Moses.

This triad partnered together in a way that symbolizes intercession. Exodus 17:12-13 says, "When Moses' hands grew tired, they took a stone and put it under him and he sat on it. Aaron and Hur held his hands up—one on one side, one on the other—so that his hands remained steady till sunset. So Joshua overcame the Amalekite army with the sword."

Moses built an altar on that hilltop and named it "The Lord our Banner" (Exodus 17:15). Whenever I read this I think of high school gymnasiums with their banners celebrating "2007 State Football Champions" or "1993 Basketball League Champions." **THEY ARE REMEMBERING THE VICTORIES OF YESTERDAY TO LAUNCH THEM INTO THE BATTLES OF TOMORROW.**

When we agree in prayer with other believers against the enemy and for the mission of God, we raise a banner of victory and **YOU CAN HEAR THE OLD QUEEN SONG BEGIN TO PLAY, "WE ARE THE CHAMPIONS!"**

Often churches or pastors will ask me, "How can we get our church moving again?" I will answer with a question, "What stopped it from advancing in the first place?" Then I hear all kinds of situations, sob stories, excuses. These are real. These are contributing factors. Many of these are significant as to why that church is failing. But not once have I heard someone say, "Because we lost our focus on prayer." Not once has someone pointed to Ephesians 6 and said "Because we took our armor off and stopped taking a spiritual stand against the evil one."

We want the the quick fix, the perfect leader, the new building, the hot worship leader, the smartest strategy, but we don't want to fall on our faces and seek God until we have a breakthrough.

CONSIDER THIS: WHY DO YOU THINK WE OFTEN SUBSTITUTE PRAYER FOR OUR OWN EFFORTS TO MAKE THINGS HAPPEN?

John Wesley emphasized the priority on prayer as the means to reach souls. His passion was to reach people without Christ. His famous statement needs to become the cry of Wesleyans once more: **"YOU HAVE NOTHING TO DO BUT TO SAVE SOULS. THEREFORE SPEND AND BE SPENT IN THIS WORK."**[23]

But Wesley understood that **TO REACH THESE SOULS HE MUST FOLLOW THE WISDOM OF EPHESIANS 6 AND STRUGGLE AGAINST SPIRITUAL FORCES OF EVIL WHICH DID NOT WANT TO SURRENDER THEM.** This was one of Wesley's reasons for rising at 4am each morning to devote himself to prayer and why his rule of life included fasting two days a week until 3pm.[24]

This powerful combination of passion for souls and priority upon prayer birthed the Methodist movement. This might not be popular today but it's not out of style with God.

CONSIDER THIS: WHAT IN YOUR MINISTRY OR CHURCH ARE YOU EARNESTLY PRAYING WILL MULTIPLY?

The Mustard Seed Tribe believes the nematodes that are diminishing the harvest and undermining multiplication can be repelled through fervent prayer if we will practice it. As the legendary Mustard Seed leader, John Wesley, taught, "God does nothing but in answer to prayer."[25]

---

23   John Telford, *"Wesley's Preachers,"* The Life of John Wesley, Wesley Center Online, http://wesley.nnu. edu/?id=96 (accessed June 24, 2016).

24   Clifton Stringer, *"John Wesley's Rule of Life,"* Ministry Matters, September 8, 2014, http://www. ministrymatters.com/all/entry/5398/john-wesleys-rule-of-life (accessed June 24, 2016).

25   John Wesley, *A Plain Account of Christian Perfection*, http://www.worldinvisible.com/library/ wesley/8317/831711.htm (accessed July 2, 2016).

QUESTIONS TO CONSIDER:

1. What has been your experience in engaging the spiritual realm of darkness?

2. How would you describe your prayer life on behalf of the mission of God?

3. In what ways do you exercise direct authority against the forces of evil?

4. Why do you think we often substitute prayer for our own efforts to make things happen?

5. What in your ministry or church are you earnestly praying will multiply?

CHAPTER ELEVEN: STICKY

WE BELIEVE
MULTIPLICATION IS MORE
CAUGHT THAN TAUGHT
AND SIMPLICITY MAKES IT
CONTAGIOUS.

PHILIPPIANS 4:9 "Whatever you have learned or received or heard from me, or seen in me--put it into practice. And the God of peace will be with you."

Paul's words to the Philippian church in Philippians 4:9 were simple – whatever you heard me say and saw me do, repeat daily. Herein lies a crucial cause of the dearth of multiplication we are seeing in America. When we hear it but don't see it, it doesn't stick.

We, the church in America, are guilty of relying on our words instead of our actions to transmit the gospel. Our training has predominately consisted of classroom lectures, books, conferences, notebooks, and Sunday sermons. We have sought to multiply disciples by telling them what to do, rather than showing them how to live. Our lives aren't sticky. **OUR METHODS AREN'T STICKY, SO THE CHURCH IS SICKLY.**

The great philosopher, Søren Kierkegaard, told a story about ducks that came from an imaginary country where only ducks live. One Sunday morning, all the mother and father ducks headed to church with their children waddling behind them. They entered the doors and sat in their duck pews, sang songs from their duck hymnals, and gave to underprivileged ducks at the offering time. When the duck preacher got up to proclaim the message, he was very dynamic. He opened his duck Bible and screamed, "Ducks, you can fly! You have wings and you can fly like eagles." The ducks all chanted, "We can fly, we can fly!" He asked, "Do you believe you can fly?" Again, they shouted back, "We can fly, we can fly." He screamed again, "We can soar through the skies!" They all shouted, "Amen." With that the pastor closed his duck Bible and dismissed his congregation of ducks. Then they all waddled back home.[26]

How should the story have ended? The duck pastor should have said, "Now come outside with me and we will have some flying lessons. Follow me. Fly with me." **THIS IS WHAT MAKES TRUTH "STICKY" AND TRANSFERABLE.**

CONSIDER THIS: IN WHAT WAYS DO YOU SEE THE CHURCH IN AMERICA PREACHING ABOUT "FLYING" WITHOUT MODELING IT?

Mustard plants multiply like crazy and spread rapidly. One of the keys to this multiplication is the stickiness of each individual seed. For example, the Sahara Mustard plant had 3-inch long seed pods that look like stiff, skinny green beans. Inside these ripe pods are round, poppy-seed size, bright red mustard seeds. One large mustard plant can produce 16,000 seeds!

---

26   Jim Burns, "*Parable of the Ducks,*" Home Word, June 6, 2016, https://homeword.com/devotionals/parable-of-the-ducks/#.V3Ey3pMrLEY (accessed June 27, 2016).

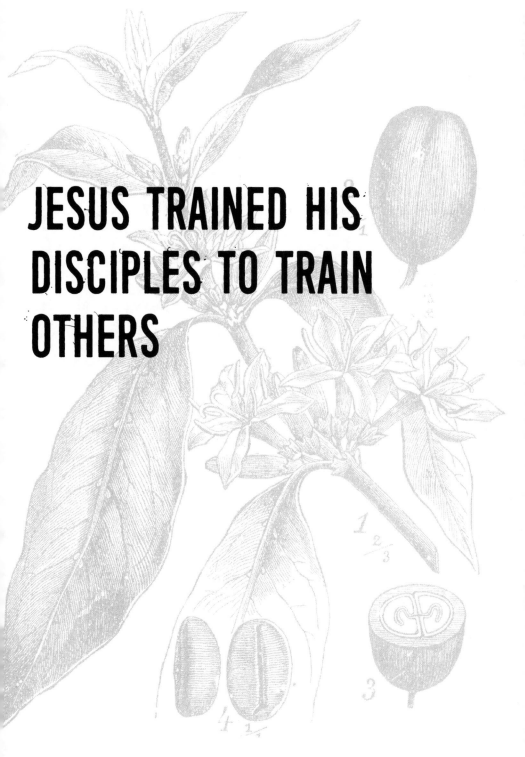

JESUS TRAINED HIS DISCIPLES TO TRAIN OTHERS

When the seed pods mature, they spring open and release their seeds. Each seed has a sticky coating so that it sticks to anything it comes in contact with - animal fur, bird feathers, shoe bottoms, clothing, vehicle tires, etc. Get almost anything close enough to it and it will stick. The seed will then be carried near and far to be propagated and multiplied.

The Mustard Seed Tribe is determined to live in sticky ways, passing on the gospel personally, through relationships, in ordinary, everyday situations. The goal of this tribe is to teach through bringing believers close enough to themselves that the message sticks because their followers have seen it, not just heard it. **THE MUSTARD SEED TRIBE WANTS TO HELP PEOPLE LIVE IT AND HELP THEM TEACH OTHERS TO LIVE IT ALSO.** Both are vital in multiplication.

This means getting out of the pulpit and into the lives of people; out of the classrooms and into the living rooms; out of the Sunday School class and into coffee shops. It encompasses teaching people to pray by spending hours in prayer with them, training them to witness by sharing your faith with someone while they watch, mentoring them in serving by sacrificing some Saturdays to fix up the home of a widow, **EQUIPPING THEM TO TEACH BY HAVING THEM HELP YOU TEACH.**

CONSIDER THIS: HOW STICKY ARE THE SERMONS AT YOUR CHURCH? WHAT MAKES THEM MORE OR LESS STICKY?

The Learning Pyramid was developed way back in the 1960s by the NTL Institute in Bethel, Maine. What the pyramid measured was the most effective means of helping people retain knowledge. While the exact research has been legitimately questioned, educators will report they have found the basic ideas it suggests to be undeniably true.

The Learning Pyramid reports that students retain:
5% of what they learn from lecture.
10% of what they learn from reading.
20% of what they learn from audio-visual.
30% of what they learn when they see a demonstration.
50% of what they learn when engaged in a group discussion.
75% of what they learn when they practice what they learned.
90% of what they learn when they teach someone else/use immediately. [27]

---

[27] *"How to Retain 90% of Everything You Learn,"* Psychotactics.com, http://www.psychotactics.com/art-retain-learning/ (accessed June 27, 2016).

To put this in our terms of multiplication, when we tell people what to do, little learning is transpiring. It's not too sticky. But when we discuss it with them, do it with them, train them to teach it to someone else, and then send them out to teach it then it gets really sticky.

Jesus used these sticky methods to train his disciples and start a movement. Jesus wasn't going to rely on verbal instruction to change lives; he was going to live with them to show them what it looked like. Then he would send them out to do it and then they discussed it. Perhaps even more importantly, **JESUS TRAINED THEM TO TRAIN OTHERS.**

CONSIDER THIS: WHO ARE YOUR MODELS FOR THE CHRISTIAN LIFE YOU ARE LIVING NOW?

I am a preacher. I believe in the power of proclaiming the Word of God. I have seen it instantaneously transform lives as the Holy Spirit convicts a person and they respond. I want to spend the rest of my life declaring God's truth in public settings. But far more importantly, I want to train disciples who will multiply themselves.

THE SEED OF THE WORD IS STICKY WHEN IT IS SIMPLIFIED TO ITS ESSENTIALS and converts are rapidly mobilized to spread it. Although classical theological training is of great value, it can become a hurdle to multiplication. It should be the desirable but optional equipment.

Too often theological education is treated as the engine or the tires or the steering wheel of the gospel vehicle. It is not. The gospel is simple. It is straightforward and transformative. The Spirit of God, using the essential truths of salvation can transform and propel people's lives. Formal theological training is the optional equipment that helps keep the car safe; it's the turn signals, the bumpers, the air bags, the mirrors, the windshield.

Consider this: In 1771, when 26-year-old Francis Asbury arrived in America, there were only 300 American Methodists, led by four ministers. **BY THE TIME OF ASBURY'S DEATH IN 1816, METHODISM HAD 2,000 MINISTERS AND OVER 200,000 MEMBERS** in a well-coordinated movement. By 1830 official membership was almost half a million, and the number of actual attenders was six million. Most of these people had no previous church connection before they became Methodists.[28]

---

28   Rodney Stark, *The Rise of Christianity: A Sociologist Reconsiders History* (Princeton, N.J.: Princeton University Press, 1996), p. 3.

The Methodists developed strategies that made it easy for gifted and committed laypeople to take up leadership and go where the people and the opportunities were. Deployment was rapid because very little upfront investment of resources and education was required. Methodist preachers, many of whom were teenagers, were trained on the job as apprentices by more experienced workers. They were expected to be continually studying as they traveled. They practiced lifelong learning and graduated the day they died.[29]

Emphasizing the gospel essentials, apprenticing new believers, and swift deployment were vital to the quick spread of the gospel through early Methodism. It is what is often referred to as "from the harvest to the harvest" priority – winning people to Christ and immediately sending them to win other for Christ. These factors created the stickiness that propelled the movement.

It is to be noted that Methodism was not anti-education. Indeed, the opposite was true. Methodists ministers and lay people were expected to be lifelong learners. But their education was to occur in the heat of battle, in the field of service, in the spread of the gospel, and in the planting of churches. Evangelism was too important to wait for education.

The Mustard Seed Tribe majors in the transforming essentials of the gospel and quickly sends disciples out to share it with others. **THIS TRIBE OPERATES IN A LOW CONTROL, HIGH ACCOUNTABILITY MANNER.**

CONSIDER THIS: HAVE YOU EVER HAD AN APPRENTICE WITH YOU IN YOUR WORKPLACE? IN YOUR MINISTRY? WHAT WAS IT LIKE FOR YOU?

MOVEMENTS ARE MESSY. They require ample freedom but also high enough accountability so the core beliefs and values are not compromised or diluted.

If the entry bar for service is set too high (i.e. transformed enough, mature enough, trained enough, educated enough, denominational enough) the movement is slowed or even halted.

29   Steve Addison, *Movements that Change the World*, Revised edition (Downers Grove, IL: InterVarsity Press, 2011) p. 90.

If the message is too complex (nuanced understanding necessary, non-essentials comprehended, breadth of understanding wide enough, denominational enough) then the majority of movement makers are sidelined.

If the structure is too sophisticated (legal hoops to jump through, insurance demands to be satisfied, denominational certification of differing levels to be accomplished, certain boards to have positioned, too many specific educational classes to have been taken) then the movement bogs down under the weight of the structure. These structures are often put in place in an effort to keep the movement "safe" but instead generally slow and kill movements.

High control diminishes stickiness. Ample freedom increases stickiness. Yet, there needs to be accountability. Not only is accountability biblical, it is advantageous for movement. **A RIVER WITHOUT BANKS BECOMES A SHALLOW LAKE THAT EVAPORATES QUICKLY.** There must be boundaries, banks, parameters. **A MOVEMENT HAS CORE BELIEFS/VALUES, AND THESE MUST BE SAFEGUARDED.** This accountability is best carried out not through creating structures of high control, but through personal relationships with apostolic authority. This is the pattern we see in the book of Acts. Great freedom, yet apostolic authority to bring correction when necessary.

"LOW CONTROL" MEANS THERE IS ROOM TO BE LED BY THE SPIRIT, to be self-expressive, and to creatively structure your ministry or church in ways that are most advantageous for the mission in your context. "High accountability" means you welcome spiritually mature men and women to evaluate and speak into your character, your message, and even your methods.

Hebrews 13:17 was written for all Christians, including Christian leaders – "Have confidence in your leaders and submit to their authority, because they keep watch over you as those who must give an account. Do this so that their work will be a joy, not a burden, for that would be of no benefit to you." It is this brand of submission that benefits multiplication of ministry.

Movements without this type of accountability are dangerous. I discovered this the hard way. In my twenties I was a youth pastor in one of the largest churches in Seattle. At 26 years of age I was preaching to 4,000 people every other month. This church had grown rapidly and started more than 20 other churches.

But it was an independent church. When the elders discovered the pastor was having multiple affairs, they requested he step down. He basically responded, "I started this church and you are all fired". Without rehearsing the details, it got ugly. The church diminished from 4,000 to 400 in four months and the movement was suddenly shifted into reverse.

The pastor was a dangerous leader because he was leading a movement from the pulpit without showing us how to do it. He wasn't providing us a model to emulate. He was isolated from the streets of ministry, too proud to serve the poor himself. He was secluded from real relationships which could keep him healthy. His message was not the simple gospel. He was without outside accountability who could correct him and safeguard the movement. He crumbled and damaged many people in his fall.

CONSIDER THIS: HOW OFTEN ARE WE BEING TAUGHT TO TEACH WHAT WE ARE LEARNING?

MULTIPLICATION THRIVES IN SETTINGS WHERE THERE IS ADEQUATE FREEDOM TO MAKE IT STICKY, BUT ENOUGH ACCOUNTABILITY TO KEEP IT TRUE.

Multiplication blossoms when it's driven by passion instead of defined by rules. The Pharisees had thousands of laws. Jesus taught two— Love God, love others. **DO THE ESSENTIALS WITH PASSION AND PASS IT ON TO SOMEONE NEAR YOU.**

In Australia there are two main methods for keeping cattle on the ranch. One is to build a fence around the perimeter. The other is to dig a well in the center of the property. Movements major in wells, not fences. **WELLS ARE STICKY; FENCES ARE NOT.** Let's dig deeper wells, not erect higher fences.

QUESTIONS TO CONSIDER:

1. Who are your models for the Christian life you are living now?

2. In what ways do you see the church in America preaching about "flying" without modeling it?

3. How sticky are the sermons at your church? What makes them more or less sticky?

4. How often are we being taught to teach what we are learning?

5. Have you ever had an apprentice with you in your workplace? In your ministry? What was it like for you?

CHAPTER TWELVE: ADAPTIVE

WE BELIEVE
MULTIPLICATION
CAN THRIVE IN ANY
ENVIRONMENT BY
CONTEXTUALIZING THE
TRUTH WITHOUT
CHANGING IT.

I CORINTHIANS 9:22-23 "To the weak I became weak, to win the weak. I have become all things to all people so that by all possible means I might save some. I do all this for the sake of the gospel, that I may share in its blessings."

In 1991 Light & Life in Long Beach was a small group of wonderful Anglo-Saxon saints (read "white") trying to do church in a neighborhood that had morphed from Dutch dairy farmers to a multi-ethnic urban population comprised of less than 20% Anglo-Saxons. The church had made a few changes along the way but basically things remained the same as when they started in 1954.

Some young leaders began to push for modifications, and they brought in radical new music like you would hear on the radio. They hired a young, inexperienced pastor who loved to make changes. Soon the praise music was fast and loud, the organ was gone, the hymnals were in the closet, the preaching style was contemporary, paint colors were modernized, carpet was replaced, Sunday School classes became discipleship groups, prayer walks through the neighborhood started, the dozen committees were disbanded and they were praying for the sick and seeing miracles happen.

CONSIDER THIS: IN WHAT WAYS HAS YOUR MINISTRY CONTEXT AND YOUR ENVIRONMENT CHANGED OVER THE PAST DECADE?

THE CHURCH WAS KNOCKING ON THE DOORS OF OUR MULTI-ETHNIC NEIGHBORS, introducing ourselves, and asking how our church could serve their needs. We didn't know it, but we were asking these questions:
1) How can we adapt our church to meet your needs?
2) How can we contextualize our ministry to meet you where you are?
3) How can we come to you instead of insisting you come to us?
4) How can we evolve to be relevant to your reality?

The results of these changes received mixed reviews. A few of the old-timers were upset and left in protest – "You have stolen our church!" "I was raised in this church and now you have messed up my church!" "I thought we were a holiness church. This music is the kind I hear at work!" "It's too loud and too fast" Meanwhile, the younger generation was loving it and inviting their friends.

Two of the elderly mothers of the church helped immensely with comments which became oft repeated and culture shaping. One, who had been there since the church began, stood up in an all-church meeting and flatly declared, "If everyone here would get busy rowing the boat you wouldn't have time to rock it!" The other, even older, saint said, "PASTOR, I DON'T LIKE THE MUSIC, BUT I LIKE SEEING PEOPLE GET SAVED. And I like seeing people get saved a whole lot more than I dislike the music. So keep it up!"

CONSIDER THIS: WHICH GENERATION IS DEFINING THE MAJORITY OF YOUR CURRENT CHURCH CULTURE?

The church adapted to the culture around it, grew dramatically, and became a multi-ethnic congregation, effectively impacting the surrounding community. The apostle Paul would have been pleased, since he did the same in his ministry (1 Corinthians 9:22-23).

Mustard plants are amazingly adaptive. Mustard can be found in deserts and in marshes, in high altitudes and low altitudes, in full shade and full light, in shallow soil and fertile soil, in most countries of the world, in all hemispheres of the globe. MUSTARD SEEDS ARE FOUND EVERYWHERE. Even King Tut's Tomb was stocked with mustard seed so he could have spice in the afterlife. Mustard seeds have been cultivated after lying dormant in the ground for sixty years.[30]

Whatever context mustard seeds find themselves in, they find a way to adapt, thrive, and begin to multiply. There are few places that mustard seeds cannot be cultivated.

What a powerful picture of the gospel. IN THE FIRST CENTURY, ROME AND JERUSALEM COULD NOT HAVE BEEN MORE DIFFERENT, YET THE GOSPEL SPREAD FROM JERUSALEM TO ROME AND WAS FLOURISHING IN JUST ONE GENERATION. This would be like planting mustard in Iceland and Fiji, two completely different environments, and both flourishing.

The Mustard Seed Tribe believes, AS LONG AS THE CORE DNA OF THE GOSPEL REMAINS UNCHANGED, IT CAN BE PLANTED ANYWHERE AND FLOURISH. It will need to, however, adapt to the climate which it is in. In gospel terms this is called "contextualization."

---

30   Clarence R. Quick, "How Long Can a Seed Remain Alive?" Yearbook of Agriculture 1961, http://fs.fed.us/psw/publications/documents/misc/yoa1961_quick001.pdf (accessed June 27, 2016).

Some mistakenly believe that **CONTEXTUALIZATION MEANS MAKING CHRISTIANITY LOOK JUST LIKE THE CULTURE.** However, contextualization is simply the process of making the gospel understood. In fact, much of what many call contextualization is simply an effort to be trendy or edgy. It may be effective, it may attract a hearing, it may not be offensive to hearers, but that is not contextualization; that is marketing.[31]

One of the foremost authorities on gospel movements, Steve Addison, says:

> To fulfill their mission, the most effective movements are prepared to change everything about themselves except their core beliefs. Unencumbered by tradition, movements feel free to experiment with new forms and strategies. Movements pursue their mission with methods that are effective, flexible, and reproducible which outlast and even surpass the influence of the first generation of leaders.[32]

No thinking person would argue the fact that we are in times of rapid change and sociological upheaval. These are times of despair for those who cannot adapt. But for those who know the power of sanctified shape-shifting, these are times of great opportunity. We must, however, become students of our particular cultures.

Futurist Alvin Toffler said, "The illiterate of the twenty first century will not be those who cannot read and write, but those who cannot learn, unlearn and relearn." Eric Hoffer wrote, "In times of drastic change, it is the learners who inherit the future. The learned find themselves well equipped to live in a world that no longer exists."[33] **THE CHURCH HAS OFTEN FAILED TO LEARN NEW WAYS OF DOING CHURCH AND CONSEQUENTLY, IS WELL-SUITED TO REACH A POPULATION THAT HAS DIED.**

When I was studying for the ministry at Azusa Pacific University, I read a book by an insightful and godly author, Howard Snyder. As I reflect back on the book, I realize this was probably the first author I had read who represented the Mustard Seed Tribe. The book was entitled The Problem of Wineskins.

Snyder took his cue from Jesus' words in Matthew 9:17: "Neither do people pour new wine into old wineskins. If they do, the skins will burst; the wine will run out and the wineskins will be ruined. No, they pour new wine into new wineskins, and both are preserved."

31 Juan Sanchez, "*To Contextualize or Not to Contextualize: That is NOT the Question*, The Gospel Coalition, December 13, 2009, https://www.thegospelcoalition.org/article/to-contextualize-or-not-to-contextualize-that-is-not-the-question (accessed June 27, 2016).
32 Steve Addison, *Movements that Change the World*, Revised edition (Downers Grove, IL: InterVarsity Press, 2011) p. 167.
33 "Eric Hoffer," *Wikipedia*, https://en.wikiquote.org/wiki/Eric_Hoffer (accessed June 28, 2016).

Snyder goes on to challenge us about our propensity to idolize wineskins and hang onto them after they have lost their usefulness. He writes convincingly that **IF WE ARE TO RECEIVE AND RETAIN THE NEW WINE WE MUST BE WILLING TO ADAPT OUR WINESKINS:**

> The church will increasingly have to choose between a charismatic and an institutional or bureaucratic model for its life and structure. Technological development, population growth and other factors are speeding up the pace of change and squeezing humanity into a potential global ghetto... This means newer, more instantly responsive forms of organization must characterize the future...Whether this is good or bad for the church depends on whether it is structured according to a charismatic or an institutional model. Biblically, it is clear that the church should be structured charismatically and organically, and any church so structured already is largely prepared to withstand future shock.[34]

It is difficult to imagine these words were originally penned in 1975. Forty years later Snyder's prophetic words have never been truer. These charismatic, organic churches have emphasized following the Spirit instead of sister Suzy's preferences. They have been willing to contextualize and change.

They've been willing to sacrifice their sacred cows and throw a barbecue for the lost. I think every disciple and church leader must continually ask themselves, **"WHAT STRUCTURE OR METHOD HAS BECOME SO COMFORTABLE OR SO VALUABLE TO ME THAT I AM UNWILLING TO SACRIFICE IT FOR THE SAKE OF THE MISSION?"** This is the Isaac question (Genesis 22:2) that is a prerequisite to being multiplied like Abraham was multiplied.

CONSIDER THIS: WHAT ARE THE SACRED COWS IN YOUR MINISTRY OR CHURCH THAT MAY NEED TO BE SACRIFICED?

Churches who have refused to adapt have suffered the old wineskin fate of going out of business or at the best being on life support waiting for the last saint to pass. A church in New York closed down and someone taped a sign to the front door: "Out of Business. Forgot what Business They Were In."

---

34   Howard Snyder, *Radical Renewal: The Problem of Wineskins Today.* Wipf & Stock Pub, 2005, p. 194.

WE DON'T SO MUCH PREACH AS WE DO LIVE OUT THE GOSPEL AMONG THE PEOPLE

Conversely, those who have adapted and compromised the truth to fit culture (read: most mainline churches) are also in steep decline. **WE MUST HOLD MORE LOOSELY ANY WINESKIN OR METHOD, WHILE HOLDING MORE TENACIOUSLY THAN EVER TO THE ESSENTIAL TRUTHS OF THE GOSPEL.**

Our church, Light and Life, has started churches or held services in all kinds of wineskins. Community centers, school auditoriums, YMCA gyms, movie theaters, recreational centers, houses, hotel banquet rooms, outside in parks, Masonic lodges, rented churches, abandoned churches, elementary school cafeterias, restaurants. With few exceptions (like strip clubs), if it holds people, we will use it. We can't, however, claim to be that innovative because, in 1957, when our church had property but no meeting space, they drove a big yellow school bus onto the dirt lot and held services in it for over a year!

Too often we approach evangelizing our nation or city like it is a flat pancake, with the same kind of people throughout. Therefore, we use the same kind of strategies or methods. But our country, states, and cities are not pancakes; they are waffles. Waffles have individual divots filled with specific types of people who can be best reached with certain kinds of tactics.

There is not one broad culture in America or in your town. Instead, there are micro-cultures. There are pockets of unique cultures with people who dress, think, play, relate in specific ways. Understanding these cultures and sending people into them is the most effective way for the church to reach those who aren't interested in typical church.

CONSIDER THIS: WHAT ARE SOME OF THE MICRO-CULTURES WITHIN A FIFTEEN-MINUTE DRIVE FROM YOUR HOUSE?

One of my heroes is Free Methodist elder, Marty Edwards. In the midst of a successful ministry career of pastoring a sizeable church and planting "normal" churches, God called him to ride a motorcycle. More accurately, God placed a heavy burden on his heart to reach a micro-culture; specifically, people who were passionate Harley Davidson motorcycle riders. Marty would have to adapt his whole style of ministry in order to bring the gospel to this particular tribe. To Marty's credit, he courageously resigned his job and started a ministry called, "Black Sheep – Harley Davidson For Christ."

Rev. Edwards writes: "I left the traditional pulpit because I found a sub-culture of people the church would never reach. Missions is not just about foreign countries, it's about groups of unreached people...**WE DON'T SO MUCH PREACH AS WE DO LIVE OUT THE GOSPEL AMONG THE PEOPLE**...'friend of sinners' Jesus said. O, we're bold, just not so obnoxious. The Sheep sincerely love the motorcycle culture."[35]

With that kind of heart and vision, it should not be surprising that Black Sheep has multiplied to most states in the nation and internationally as well. They are contextualizing the gospel to a micro-culture that has been largely unreached and would remain so if left up to the old wineskin, traditional church.

While contextualization is vital, we must not allow it to distort the reality that at the core people are the same. People tend to pursue individuality while in various ways demonstrating their similarities. All kinds of people go to Starbucks but once there they personalize their drinks. Their coffee craving seeks fulfillment, but they want to do it their way.

All people—those who ride horses, Harleys, surfboards, elephants, camels, BMWs, and buses—crave Jesus. **THERE IS AN UNDENIABLE, YET OFTEN UNCONSCIOUS DESIRE TO LIVE IN RELATIONSHIP WITH THE LIVING GOD.** They wish for immortality. They long for true friends. They yearn for purpose in their life and to leave a legacy. They seek love, joy, and peace. In these ways people are all the same. Only God's truth empowered by the Spirit through the church can meet these needs.

CONSIDER THIS: ARE YOU SEEKING TO MULTIPLY ONLY MINISTRIES WHICH LOOK LIKE YOURS, OR ARE YOU EMPOWERING CREATIVE MINISTRIES UNLIKE YOURS?

The first characteristic of God mentioned in the Bible is creativity. His Spirit hovered over the chaos of the murky, churning waters. Then our creative God spoke and an innovative element came into existence – light! The darkness was disrupted, overcome and pushed back. Something beautiful began to arise from the disorder (Genesis 1:1-3).

---

35   Marty Edwards, "*Why Black Sheep Mentors Members*," Black Sheep: Harley Davidsons for Christ Newsletter, June 2016, http://www.blacksheephdfc.org/images/newsletters/bshdfc-jun%202016.pdf (accessed June 28, 2016).

Our society is a churning ocean of ideologies, differing moralities, hedonism, perversity, injustice and idolatry. But God is not absent. He is hovering. He is here. He is longing to bring something beautiful out of these dark times.

As the church we must not compromise but we must be creative. Our ability to adapt without acquiescing; to be incarnational and not isolating; to be inventive without being faddish; this is what will allow us to be the light of the world Jesus is calling us to be. This light multiplies.

QUESTIONS TO CONSIDER:

1. In what ways has your ministry context and your environment changed over the past decade?

2. What are some of the micro-cultures within a fifteen-minute drive from your house?

3. Which generation is defining the majority of your current church culture?

4. What are the sacred cows in your ministry or church that may need to be sacrificed?

5. Are you seeking to multiply only ministries which look like yours, or are you empowering creative ministries unlike yours?

CHAPTER THIRTEEN: WIND

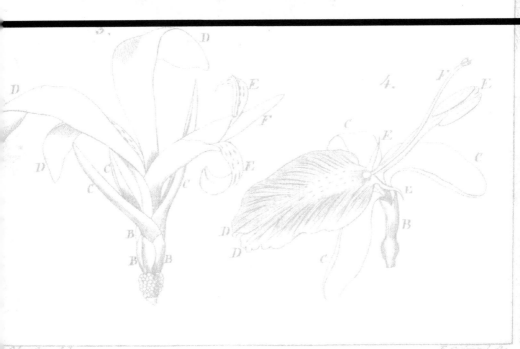

Tab. V.

WE BELIEVE IN A RADICAL DEPENDENCE UPON THE SPIRIT'S POWER TO MULTIPLY MINISTRY.

ACTS 1:8 "But you will receive power when the Holy Spirit comes on you; and you will be my witnesses in Jerusalem, and in all Judea and Samaria, and to the ends of the earth."

I was nervous. I had only been in the Free Methodist family for a few years when the Bishops asked me to Atlanta to lead them in an evening of prayer. Coming from an independent church background, I was still learning who the Free Methodists really were. I feared saying something ignorant or offensive.

At the same time, I sincerely wanted to influence the denomination towards more of the power of the Holy Spirit. It was why they had asked me to craft this prayer time. As the evening unfolded, **THE SPIRIT HELPED ME OVERCOME MY FEAR** and be open to what He may share through me.

I am one who rarely sees visions, but that evening I received a vision from God. In the vision we were in a room similar to the one our meeting was being held in that evening, except the ceilings of the room were 30 feet high. Also, strikingly, in the middle of the room was a very large, heavily ornamented, golden birdcage. Inside was a stunning white dove, softly cooing.

There was a group of denominational leaders standing around the cage, admiring the impressive beauty of the dove. Some were describing it in minute detail. Others were imagining it flying and describing what it looked like. Some were simply praising its exquisite appearance. Others were standing back from the cage as if they feared getting too close to such a magnificent bird.

In the vision I began to weep and intercede in prayer. **THERE WAS SOMETHING DREADFULLY WRONG WITH WHAT I WAS SEEING.** As I pressed deeper in prayer, the vision continued, and someone whom I couldn't see stopped talking, walked over to the cage, and decisively threw open the door. The dove immediately flapped its wings, flew from the cage and began to gently, yet powerfully, circle over the group.

The vision concluded. I was immediately hit with the question of whether I would share it with these prestigious leaders. I did. They responded with humility, desire, and prayer.

CONSIDER THIS: HOW MUCH EMPHASIS IS PLACED UPON THE SPIRIT'S WORK IN YOUR MINISTRY AND CHURCH?

THE RESULT OF THE SPIRIT'S POWER IS BOLDNESS IN SPREADING THE GOSPEL MESSAGE

For the past two decades I have been sharing this vision in various settings. It is noble to study the Holy Spirit, admire his power, and write theology about his virtue and abilities. There is, however, a danger in doing so, a danger we often succumb to. I call it "domesticating the dove." As C.S. Lewis writes concerning Christ, "Aslan is not a tame lion." I would add, "The Holy Spirit is not a domestic dove."

Unless we uncage the Holy Spirit, we will never know the power of the Spirit. **OUR THEOLOGY CAN BE CORRECT EVEN AS WE LIVE WITH A CAGED BIRD,** and the resultant feebleness. The most consistent evidence of the Spirit's fullness in the book of Acts is boldness to speak God's truth.

The Mustard Seed Tribe believes, although we are small in ourselves, **THE POWER OF THE SPIRIT GIVES US SUPERNATURAL ABILITY TO WITNESS WITH POWER AND MULTIPLY THE MINISTRIES WE ARE IN.**

CONSIDER THIS: WHAT IS YOUR CURRENT LEVEL OF BOLDNESS IN SHARING CHRIST WITH OTHERS?

Our daily attention needs to be riveted on the final words of Jesus before his ascension. **THESE WORDS OF MISSION AND EMPOWERMENT DIRECT AND EQUIP US.** Acts 1:8: "But you will receive power when the Holy Spirit comes on you; and you will be my witnesses..."

Our theology informs us that, upon us being born again, **WE ARE INDWELT BY THE HOLY SPIRIT.** It seems we become content with this truth without expecting the reality of it to ever burst out in power. It is as if we settle for the daily low voltage current that keeps the lights on, with little anticipation of brilliant flashes of lightening.

Growing up on the farm in Kansas, I was often installing and crossing electric fences. Some were so low voltage I could grab them with my bare hand with nothing more than a tingle. Others were so highly charged that touching them with my bare hand nearly knocked me to my bottom.

Being filled with the Spirit calls us to believe for both types of empowerment. We need the low voltage flow of the Spirit that powers us through the daily routines of life with a strength beyond our own. But we also need to believe for uncommon displays of the supernatural. **WE CAN'T LIVE ON LIGHTENING, BUT WE CAN EXPECT IT TO PIERCE THE DARKNESS IN MOMENTARY FLASHES.**

I vividly recall, during one church service at Light & Life, inviting the Holy Spirit to manifest himself in healing. One woman who came down to receive prayer for healing had not walked without the aid of her cane for several years. As the church prayed she felt an electric shock down her leg and she dropped the cane and began to dance around the front. She told me her adult son was so moved by watching this, he placed his faith in Christ that night.

CONSIDER THIS: ARE YOU OPEN TO MANIFESTATIONS OF THE SPIRIT IN HEALING, MIRACLES, AND DELIVERANCE?

Some of the same people in Acts 2 who got "zapped" with the Holy Spirit were there again in Acts 4 and were shaken up by the Spirit. Acts 4:31 describes it this way: "After they prayed, the place where they were meeting was shaken. And they were all filled with the Holy Spirit and spoke the word of God boldly."

In Acts 2 and then in Acts 4 **THE RESULT OF THE SPIRIT'S POWER WAS BOLDNESS IN SPREADING THE GOSPEL MESSAGE.** Sometimes people with certain gifts or others who feel they've attained a certain level of sanctification want to instruct me on what the "real" filling of the Spirit looks like.

My first question back to them is always, "How has this changed the way you share the gospel and demonstrate its power to unbelievers?" The genuine anointing of the Spirit in the book of Acts led to unflinching and valiant witnessing, just like Jesus promised in Acts 1:8.

AN UTTER DEPENDENCY UPON THE HOLY SPIRIT TO SPREAD THE SEED OF THE WORD AND MULTIPLY OUR MINISTRY CANNOT BE OVEREMPHASIZED.

Jesus likened the Spirit to the wind. In John 3:8 Jesus instructs us, "The wind blows wherever it pleases. You hear its sound, but you cannot tell where it comes from or where it is going. So it is with everyone born of the Spirit." Among other truths, **"UNCAGING THE DOVE" MEANS A WILLINGNESS TO BE CARRIED ON THE CURRENTS OF SPIRIT TO PLACES AND PEOPLE WHO NEED A "POWERFUL WITNESS"** (Acts 1:8).

How long has it been since you arose in the morning with an exciting anticipation that God was going to "blow" you to someone in need of your witness?

CONSIDER THIS: DO YOU CONSISTENTLY AND EARNESTLY INVITE THE HOLY SPIRIT TO FILL YOU AND GUIDE YOU?

One of the primary means of multiplication of the mustard plant is to be carried by the breeze to wherever the wind is blowing. This occurs in two ways. When the seed pods are mature they pop open and gusts bear the seeds a distance away.

Secondly, the whole mustard plant can mature, dry out, and break off at the root. The entire plant then is propelled forward by the wind. As it tumbles down the road or across the field, it scatters its seeds, sometimes for miles. When I read the Book of Acts this is the image that comes to mind, the Spirit blowing his messengers across Asia Minor.

One Biblical picture of multiplication that grips my imagination and stirs my faith is found in Ezekiel 37. The prophet Ezekiel is taken to a valley of bleached, dismembered skeletons. The first command Ezekiel receives is to tell the bones, "I will make breath enter you, and you will come to life" (Ezekiel 37:5). The bones clack, clatter, rattld, and reattaed. Muscles and tendons re-form on the bones. Yet, there is no heartbeat, no lungs breathing.

God's second command is, "Prophesy to the breath; prophesy, son of man, and say to it, 'This is what the Sovereign Lord says: Come, breath, from the four winds and breathe into these slain, that they may live'" (Ezekiel 37:9). Although the scripture does not state it, undoubtedly **THE WIND BEGINS TO BLOW, THE SPIRIT BEGINS TO MOVE ACROSS THE VALLEY FLOOR, AND INDIVIDUALS BEGIN TO STAND TO THEIR FEET.** In the end Ezekiel sees not just people, but soldiers, a vast army ready to defeat the enemy and claim kingdom territory.

This is the wind we need, the breath we long for. Some of our church people are dead, dry, and ugly. Others look good but they are lying down, without life, incapable of being sent by the Spirit. We must urgently call on the wind, the breath of the Spirit to empower these bones. It is no coincidence the Day of Pentecost in Acts 2 starts with the sound a mighty rushing wind in the upper room--**GOD'S ARMY OF LOVE IS BEING RAISED UP!**

We must again raise the cry of Ezekiel. **WE MUST PLEAD IN EARNEST DAILY PRAYER, "COME, BREATH, FROM THE FOUR WINDS AND BREATHE...!"** Anything less indicates an overreliance upon our own skills, strength and strategies. Anything less is caging the dove.

Dave was a socially awkward, shy young adult who saw conversation as a social torture device. He was a follower of Jesus with a humdrum, inconsequential walk with Christ. At a retreat we held, Dave had a deep encounter with the Holy Spirit. It transformed him. Coming down the mountain Dave determined to make daily empowerment a priority in his life. He committed to share Jesus with someone every day.

Dave's life was dramatically different. "Bold but not obnoxious" was the best way to describe the new Dave. Sure, he still needed some coaching, but his life became fruitful in inexplicable ways. Several non-Christians came to faith. Many Christians caught his fire. His life of faith was multiplying in others.

Three years later, Dave was diagnosed with brain cancer and deteriorated quickly. All through his rapid journey to the grave, Dave's chief concern was giving witness to the resurrection. I remember at his funeral gazing out on the grassy cemetery hillside, seeing dozens of changed lives and thinking, **"SO THIS IS WHAT HAPPENS WHEN WE LET THE WIND BLOW."**

CONSIDER THIS: IN WHAT WAYS CAN YOU MAKE YOURSELF MORE AVAILABLE TO THE HOLY SPIRIT?

Mustard seeds are not immediately spicy, but they have the potential to be so. They must be immersed to release the power. The enzyme myrosine gives mustard its pungent flavor. This zesty enzyme isn't activated until it's submersed in a liquid.

The Romans were probably the first to experiment with the preparation of mustard as a condiment. They mixed unfermented grape juice (the must) with ground mustard seeds to make "burning must," mustum ardens in Latin — hence "must ard."[36] Likewise, **UNLESS WE AS DISCIPLES ARE MIXED WITH THE NEW WINE OF THE SPIRIT, WE WILL NEVER RELEASE THE INFLUENCE THE WORLD NEEDS.**

---

36   "Mustard (condiment)," *Wikipedia*, https://en.wikipedia.org/wiki/Mustard_(condiment) (accessed June 30, 2016).

MULTIPLICATION OF MINISTRY IS FUELED BY THE HOLY SPIRIT, not human effort and ingenuity. Yes, there must be a vision, a strategy, a priority, and a discipline towards multiplication. Those are, however, as useless as an empty glove unless of the hand of God fills them with his divine ability.

For several years I owned a 28-foot sailboat on the coast of California. Remember, I grew up on the plains of Kansas. My sailing experience was limited to flying a kite. A co-worker of my wife owned the boat and was convinced we should purchase it. I countered, "How could I buy a sailboat when I didn't know how to sail?" He, unfazed by naiveté, responded, "There's nothing to it. I can teach you in an hour." Twenty minutes later I purchased a sailboat with one lesson as a bonus.

The sailor instructed me: "There are only two essential rules in sailing: Rule #1: Don't hit anything hard. Rule #2: Raise your sails if you want to catch the wind." The first rule would prevent sinking. The second would get you were you wanted to go.

Then he stated something that has stuck with me since. **"YOU CAN'T MAKE THE WIND BLOW BUT YOU CAN SURE MISS IT WHEN IT DOES."** I've often missed the wind of the Spirit because my faith was not positioned to catch it.

My prayer is we live with full sails up and we teach others to sail. **THIS IS THE KEY TO MULTIPLYING MINISTRY.**

QUESTIONS TO CONSIDER:

1. How much emphasis is placed upon the Spirit's work in your ministry and church?

2. What is your current level of boldness in sharing Christ with others?

3. Are you open to manifestations of the Spirit in healing, miracles, and deliverance?

4. Do you consistently and earnestly invite the Holy Spirit to fill you and guide you?

5. In what ways can you make yourself more available to the Holy Spirit?

FINAL WORD:

Having ministered for forty years and watched hundreds of churches and ministries of all types, I am convinced of this – Multiplication is not about "how" but about "why." **MULTIPLICATION IS 90% HEART AND 10% HEAD.**

IF YOUR HEART CATCHES FIRE FOR KINGDOM EXPANSION THROUGH MULTIPLICATION, YOU WILL USUALLY FIND THE BEST STRATEGY TO MAKE IT HAPPEN. Conversely, the right plan without real passion and relying on the Spirit's power will leave you trudging circles in the ministry wilderness.

Your ministry culture is far more potent than the strategy you choose. Strategy is vital, but **STRATEGY DOES NOT CREATE CULTURE.** Values do. Passion does. Action does. The Spirit does. Faith does. Risk does. Prayer does. Love does.

Often people want me to tell them how our church has multiplied leaders, ministries, and churches. They aren't looking for spiritual answers; they are looking for action plans, methods, secrets. I usually end up disappointing them. I point them to something small in the eyes of the world. **I PULL OUT A MUSTARD SEED AND TALK ABOUT ITS GREAT POWER TO MULTIPLY.**

I revisited my small friend, the mustard seed. I apologized to her for being so skeptical in our first encounter.

She graciously forgave me and went to explain, "Most people are my size and therefore, discount their ability to impact the world. What they fail to see is what can happen in just a few generations if they will multiply. **SMALL ACTS OF LOVE MULTIPLIED MANY TIMES IN MANY LIVES CAN MOVE MANY MOUNTAINS.** Our movement can reach the world."

I thanked her and began to describe in detail the Mustard Seed Tribe I had recently devoted myself to. While I was speaking with her, she was joined by two... four... eight...sixteen...thirty-two... sixty four...

FINAL THOUGHT

Knowing God is the highest priority of humanity, because knowing God changes us. We hope that this issue has given you a fresh perspective and equipped you with the raw materials God can use to keep you learning the Way of Jesus.

Sincerely,
Dr. David McDonald
Editor, FreeMo Journals

DISCIPLE DEEPLY
BY DR. DAVID MCDONALD WITH MARK VAN VALIN

The original twelve disciples were thickheaded, ego-driven, and blind; so, clearly, you don't have to be perfect in order to follow Jesus. But it seems like we give ourselves too much leeway to behave poorly, to think sloppily, or to interact disingenuously. because "nobody's perfect" we don't put a lot of effort into the process of our ongoing perfection.

We ought to change that.

EMBRACE ALL
BY JOANNA DEWOLF

The best stories only get better over time and nothing captures our hearts like the story of Jesus' birth.

HONORING FRUITFULNESS
BY RICK CALLAHAN

Jesus offers an abundant life–a life that is deep and wide, full of meaning and purpose.

CULTIVATING HEALTH
BY CHERYL WAYMAN

Why is it so hard to heal our broken relationships? How can God transform not only our relationships but out emotions as well?

PARTNER STRONG
BY BEN REDMOND

Partnership is not an optional endeavor for those of us who follow Jesus. God has placed us in this exact moment of human history, and He has chosen us as His partners. Not based on our resume or talent. No, God picks His partners based on availability over ability.

So now it's our turn to partner with God, with each other, and with the world as we find our place in the greatest story of them all.

The FreeMo Journal is published 5 times each year (Fall, Christmas, January, Easter, and Summer). Subscriptions are available through Light + Life Communication and previous issues can be ordered from The Wesleyan Publishing House at (800) 493.7539.

IF YOU'RE INTERESTED IN WRITING FOR THE FREEMO JOURNAL, PLEASE CONTACT DAVID.MCDONALD@FMCUSA.ORG